275622

▢ Contents

U. A. Fanthorpe

Tony Harrison

LONGMAN LITERATURE

Five Modern Poets

Fleur Adcock
U. A. Fanthorpe
Tony Harrison
Anne Stevenson
Derek Walcott

Editor: Barbara Bleiman

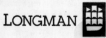
LONGMAN

Longman Literature

Series editor: Roy Blatchford

Novels

Short stories

Poetry

Anne Stevenson

Derek Walcott   113

Glossary: reading the poems   148

Working on the anthology   160

About the poets

Fleur Adcock

Fleur Adcock was born in New Zealand in 1934. She was educated in both England and New Zealand and went to Victoria University, Wellington, where she obtained a first class degree in Classics. She was married young, to a poet named Alistair Campbell. She had two sons but was divorced by the age of twenty-four. In 1963 she emigrated to Britain with her youngest son and has made her home in London. She has written: 'The question of my nationality has always seemed at least as significant as the question of my gender.'

Fleur Adcock worked as a Librarian in the Civil Service from 1959 to 1979, when she became a freelance writer. Of poetry, she has written that her classical education gave her 'respect for what is classical and based on traditions: there must be a structure; and there must always be layers of meaning, chimes and echoes and unlikely hints of other things, to be found on second or third reading'. She has also said that she finds 'understatement generally more telling than rhetorical exaggeration' and admires 'poetry which can wear a formal dress lightly and naturally'.

She has published verse translations of medieval Latin poets and two modern Romanian poets, as well as collections of her own poetry including *Tigers* (1967), *High Tide in the Garden* (1971), *The Scenic Route* (1974), *The Inner Harbour* (1979), *Below Loughrigg* (1979) and *Time Zones* (1991). Her *Selected Poems* was published by Oxford University Press in 1983 and re-issued to include new poems in 1991. She has held several literary fellowships.

U. A. Fanthorpe

U. A. Fanthorpe is a British poet, born in Kent in 1929. She was educated at Oxford and taught at Cheltenham Ladies College before becoming a 'middle-aged drop-out', taking temporary jobs, being on the dole and then, between 1974 and 1983, working as a clerical worker in a Bristol hospital. Since then she has won scholarships and has worked as a writer, taking up literary fellowships at St Martin's College Lancaster and at the Universities of Durham and Newcastle-upon-Tyne. She now lives in Gloucestershire, working as a freelance writer.

She has described herself as a 'slow learner', who came to write poetry late because she imagined that one had to experience life first. It was working as a hospital clerk/receptionist that finally led her to write poetry. Watching the patients' cheerfulness despite long waits and hospital red tape, she saw herself as a 'witness'. She felt, 'If I didn't write about what I saw, nobody else would know about it.'

Of her poetry she says, 'My poems are mostly, in one way or another, an attempt to deal with an area of darkness in my mind. I'm not able to shed light on the darkness, but it seems important to try. When the poems don't work, it is generally because of a bad habit of putting cheap wit before love.'

She has five published individual collections of poetry (all published by Peterloo Poets): *Side Effects* (1978), *Standing To* (1982), *Voices Off* (1984), *A Watching Brief* (1987) and *Neck-Verse* (1992). In 1986, a *Selected Poems* was published simultaneously by Peterloo Poets (hardback) and King Penguin (paperback).

A tape cassette of U. A. Fanthorpe introducing and reading her poems is available from Peterloo Poets.

Tony Harrison

Tony Harrison was born in Leeds, Yorkshire, in 1937, into a working-class family. He has said of his childhood in Leeds that 'In our street in Hoggarty Leeds I was the only one who used his literacy to read books, the only "scholar"; and so every kind of cultural throwaway from spring-cleaned attics and the cellars of the deceased found its way to me.' He won a scholarship to Leeds Grammar School and read Classics at the University of Leeds. Of his school he has said, 'My school, Leeds Grammar School, to which I won one of six scholarships for the plebs, seemed to me like a class conspiracy.'

He spent four years working in Nigeria and a year in Prague, before returning to England to become the first Northern Arts Fellow in Poetry at the Universities of Newcastle-upon-Tyne and Durham. He held this post twice, in 1967–8 and 1976–7. Interestingly this was a post that was also held by Anne Stevenson and U. A. Fanthorpe during their literary careers. He has won many awards for his poetry, including the UNESCO Fellowship in Poetry which allowed him to travel to Cuba, Brazil, Senegal and The Gambia.

His published anthologies include **The Loiners** (1970), **The School of Eloquence** (1978) and **Continuous** (1982). He is also a writer of dramatic verse, libretti for opera and verse translations of classical texts such as **The Oresteia** which was performed at the National Theatre.

Some of his poetry and plays have caused major public controversy. His long poem 'v', which was performed on television, was greeted with outrage from some quarters and acclaim from others. He has been accused of obscenity by some, has been attacked for being too political a poet and at the same time has won major awards, such as the Geoffrey Faber Memorial Prize (1972) and the European Poetry Translation Prize (1983).

Harrison now spends three months every year in Florida, living in a wooden shack surrounded by swamps, near the Suwannee river. His other home is in Newcastle.

Anne Stevenson

Anne Stevenson was born in England of American parents, in 1933. When she was six months old her parents went back to the USA and she was brought up in New England and Ann Arbor, Michigan. Her father taught philosophy and mathematics and was a pianist and music lover. She studied music and languages at university in Michigan before returning to England to marry a childhood playmate whom she had met in New Haven, Connecticut, during the war. The marriage was not a success and she returned to America with her four-year-old daughter in the early 1960s.

She married again and returned to England with her second husband but could not settle easily into his life as a Cambridge academic. She moved first to Glasgow and then Dundee and tried unsuccessfully to piece together her second marriage before finally moving to Hay-on-Wye, where she started 'The Poetry Bookshop' with Michael Farley, setting up a new life for herself.

In 1981–2 she was appointed Northern Arts Literary Fellow and moved to Sunderland, then County Durham. In 1987 she became writer in residence at the University of Edinburgh.

In an interview in 1989 she said, 'Poetry is the result of intense concentration. I cannot write anything at all if I have a social life, if I am pretending to be somebody I'm not, or if I'm concerned with images or personalities or any of the sort of media promoted activities which are so popular today. So in so far as I have authority, it is, I suppose, having the courage, to believe, to retreat and write what I feel I have to write. Again this comes with a certain amount of battling through the world, finding a way that is possible to live with integrity.' She has also said that she herself admires 'what is controlled, finely wrought yet passionate.'

Her published collections of poetry include *Correspondences* (1974), *Travelling Behind Glass* (1974), *Enough of Green* (1977), *Minute by Glass Minute* (1982), *The Fiction Makers* (1985) and *The Other House* (1990). Her *Selected Poems* was published in 1987.

Derek Walcott

Derek Walcott was born in Castries, St Lucia in 1930. His father died when he was only a year old. His mother was headmistress of an infant school and was a Methodist living in an overwhelmingly Catholic community. His father's father had been white, with roots in Warwickshire in England. Of his mixed race he has said, 'Mongrel that I am, something prickles in me when I see the word Ashanti as with the word Warwickshire, both separately intimating my grandfathers' roots, both baptising this neither proud nor ashamed bastard, this hybrid West Indian.'

His mixed race, his religion and his education and love of English and English literature set him apart from the French patois speaking community where he lived. He has described his background as 'a genteel, self-denying Methodist poverty', with his mother taking in sewing to pay for her sons to go through college. He studied at the University of the West Indies, Jamaica, then taught for a while before becoming a journalist on the *Trinidad Guardian.*

Walcott has won much acclaim for his poetry and plays and has travelled widely, reading his poetry and lecturing. He has spent a lot of time in the USA, teaching at the Universities of Columbia, Yale and Harvard. He is now a citizen of Trinidad and Tobago and divides his time between Trinidad and Boston, where he is Professor of English.

Interviewed about his poetry, he has said, 'A lot of modern poetry is like having corns. It hurts. It's tight and small ... What I mean is to be barefoot in spirit . . . I think if that doesn't happen poetry dies.'

Of language he has said, 'when you enter language, you enter a kind of choice which contains in it the political history of the language, the imperial width of the language, the fact that you're either subjugated by the language or you have had to dominate it. So language is not a place of retreat, it's not a place of escape, it's not even a place of resolution. It's a place of struggle.'

ABOUT THE POETS

Walcott has won many awards, including the Queen's Medal for Poetry in 1988, and his epic poem Omeros, published in 1990, won the W.H. Smith Literary Prize. In 1992 he received the Nobel Prize for Literature. He has published numerous collections of poems, including *In a Green Night* (1962). *The Castaway and Other Poems* (1965). *The Gulf* (1970), *Another Lift* (1972), *Sea Grapes* (1976). *The Stanapple Kingdom* (1979), *The Fourtunate Traveller* (1982), *Midsummer* (1982), *The Arkansas Testament* (1987) and *Omeros* (1990). His *Collected Poems* 1948-84 was published in 1986.

■ Working on a poet

■ Make a chart while you are reading, to help you identify themes and issues which seem important in the poems of the poet you are reading. When you finish reading a particular poem, try to place it on your chart or amend your chart in the light of that poem. This should help you to see patterns across poems. Your chart could be organised in different ways. If you find it useful you could keep more than one diagram going during your reading, e.g. for Derek Walcott:

THEME	Poetry	
POEMS	Mass Man	
	The Harvest	
	Midsummer (L)	
	Cul de Sac Valley (I)	

Charts like this will help you to have a broad sense of a poet's particular concerns and qualities.

Some themes you may find explored in the anthology:

PARENTHOOD   LOVE/SEX   CHANGING ONE'S COUNTRY
THE SEARCH FOR IDENTITY   POETRY   LITERATURE
CHILDHOOD   PLACES   MEMORY   TIME   LOSS   AGEING
BEING FEMALE   MALE/FEMALE RELATIONSHIPS   DEATH
MUSIC   LIFE IN THE TWENTIETH CENTURY
ENGLAND/BRITAIN   HISTORY   CULTURE   SOCIAL CLASS
COLONIALISM   THE NATURAL WORLD   FEARS
DREAMS AND NIGHTMARES

This list should help to spark off ideas but it is not exhaustive. Choose your own words or phrases to describe the themes you find in the poems, or adapt those on the list to make them fit more closely your view of the poems.

2   For a *deeper* exploration of individual poems or particular themes, this is a list of possible approaches. Adopting varied approaches will help you to develop your ability to read, talk about and write about poems in depth.

- Look at the title of the poem first. Talk about what it suggests to you.

- Read the poems aloud, rather than just in your head and read them more than once. Reading aloud might involve: one member of a small group reading aloud to the rest of the group; or a reading aloud to the whole class; or working on the poem with a partner to prepare a shared reading aloud for other students.

- Write jottings in a notebook or, if possible, around the poem itself, recording impressions and ideas. Look for something to latch on to, such as: contrasts; parallels; tensions; moments of change in the poem; recurring words, phrases, images or ideas; the mood of the poem; who is talking? to whom?

- Re-structure the poem to see what difference it makes. Why did the poet choose to put the lines where he/she did?

- Explore the importance of particular lines/words by removing or replacing them with words of your own. What difference does this make?

- Consider the poem in the light of other poems by that poet. Are there recurrent types of language, images or approaches?

- Prepare a performance of the poem. Make decisions about tone of voice, rhythm, how many voices to use and whether actions or props would help you. This is a way of making judgements about the poem and of getting to know individual poems very well.

Cultural, historical and literary references

As you will see from the glossary, many of the poems in this anthology make references to other literature and aspects of our world culture with which you may not be familiar. For instance Derek Walcott, U. A. Fanthorpe and Tony Harrison all refer to Greek and Roman mythology which played a part in shaping their thinking and their poetry.

You will need to develop strategies for dealing with such references. First of all you need to make a decision about what kind of finding out you need to do. Do you need to:

1 find out as speedily and efficiently as possible about references which obscure meaning for you; or

2 follow up in more detail any references that you become particularly interested in, or which seem to be of greater importance to the poet's work, or to your A Level studies in general?

To find quick answers to questions:
- use the glossary in the back of this book;
- share your knowledge as a group;
- make use of your teacher(s), including teachers in other subjects;
- ask friends or family;
- make use of reference books.

Useful books to have in the classroom, to buy for yourself or find in the library are:
- a dictionary;
- the Bible;
- *The Penguin Book of Quotations;*
- *Who's Who in the Ancient World,* Betty Radice (Penguin Reference);
- *Who's Who in the Bible,* Peter Calvocoressi (Penguin Dictionaries);
- *The Fontana Dictionary of Modern Thought;*
- an atlas.

More detailed research might involve you in reading more widely.

An example of researching a reference

'A Kumquat for John Keats' by Tony Harrison

The note on page 153 tells you a bit about John Keats and the fact that Harrison's poem refers to two of Keats' 'Odes'. Having read the note, you might read the two 'Odes' for yourself, to help you to understand the references. Reading around the text by following up references also means that you will read more widely and experience a range of texts, from different periods and contexts.

Five Modern Poets

Fleur Adcock

For a Five-Year-Old

A snail is climbing up the window-sill
Into your room, after a night of rain.
You call me in to see, and I explain
That it would be unkind to leave it there:
It might crawl to the floor; we must take care
That no one squashes it. You understand,
And carry it outside, with careful hand,
To eat a daffodil.

I see, then, that a kind of faith prevails:
Your gentleness is moulded still by words
From me, who have trapped mice and shot wild birds,
From me, who drowned your kittens, who betrayed
Your closest relatives, and who purveyed
The harshest kind of truth to many another.
But that is how things are: I am your mother,
And we are kind to snails.

Parting Is Such Sweet Sorrow

The room is full of clichés – 'Throw me a crumb'
And 'Now I see the writing on the wall'
And 'Don't take umbrage, dear.' I wish I could.
Instead I stand bedazzled by them all,

Longing for shade. Belshazzar's fiery script
Glows there, between the prints of tropical birds,
In neon lighting, and the air is full
Of crumbs that flash and click about me. Words

Glitter in colours like those gaudy prints:
The speech of a computer, metal-based
But feathered like a cloud of darts. All right.
Your signal-system need not go to waste.

Mint me another batch of tokens: say
'I am in your hands; I throw myself upon
Your mercy, casting caution to the winds.'
Thank you; there is no need to go on.

Thus authorised by your mechanical
Issue, I lift you like a bale of hay,
Open the window wide, and toss you out;
And gales of laughter whirl you far away.

Bogyman

Stepping down from the blackberry bushes
he stands in my path: Bogyman.
He is not as I had remembered him,
though he still wears the broad-brimmed hat,
the rubber-soled shoes and the woollen gloves.
No face; and that soft mooning voice
still spinning its endless distracting yarn.

But this is daylight, a misty autumn
Sunday, not unpopulated
by birds. I can see him in such colours
as he wears – fawn, grey, murky blue –
not all shadow-clothed, as he was that night
when I was ten; he seems less tall
(I have grown) and less muffled in silence.

I have no doubt at all, though, that he is
Bogyman. He is why children
do not sleep all night in their tree-houses.
He is why, when I had pleaded
to spend a night on the common, under
a cosy bush, and my mother
surprisingly said yes, she took no risk.

He was the risk I would not take; better
to make excuses, to lose face,
than to meet the really faceless, the one
whose name was too childish for us
to utter – 'murderers' we talked of, and
'lunatics escaped from Earlswood'.
But I met him, of course, as we all do.

Well, that was then; I survived; and later
survived meetings with his other
forms, bold or pathetic or disguised – the
slummocking figure in a dark
alley, or the lover turned suddenly
icy-faced; fingers at my throat
and ludicrous violence in kitchens.

I am older now, and (I tell myself,
circling carefully around him
at the far edge of the path, pretending
I am not in fact confronted)
can deal with such things. But what, Bogyman,
shall I be at twice my age? (At
your age?) Shall I be grandmotherly, fond

suddenly of gardening, chatty with
neighbours? Or strained, not giving in,
writing for *Ambit* and hitch-hiking to
Turkey? Or sipping Guinness in
the Bald-Faced Stag, in wrinkled stockings? Or
(and now I look for the first time
straight at you) something like you, Bogyman?

A Surprise in the Peninsula

When I came in that night I found
the skin of a dog stretched flat and
nailed upon my wall between the
two windows. It seemed freshly killed –
there was blood at the edges. Not
my dog: I have never owned one,
I rather dislike them. (Perhaps
whoever did it knew that.) It
was a light brown dog, with smooth hair;
no head, but the tail still remained.
On the flat surface of the pelt
was branded the outline of the
peninsula, singed in thick black
strokes into the fur: a coarse map.
The position of the town was
marked by a bullet-hole; it went
right through the wall. I placed my eye
to it, and could see the dark trees
outside the house, flecked with moonlight.
I locked the door then, and sat up
all night, drinking small cups of the
bitter local coffee. A dog
would have been useful, I thought, for
protection. But perhaps the one
I had been given performed that
function; for no one came that night,
nor for three more. On the fourth day
it was time to leave. The dog-skin
still hung on the wall, still and dry
by now, the flies and the smell gone.

Could it, I wondered, have been meant
not as a warning, but a gift?
And, scarcely shuddering, I drew
the nails out and took it with me.

Happy Ending

After they had not made love
she pulled the sheet up over her eyes
until he was buttoning his shirt:
not shyness for their bodies – those
they had willingly displayed – but a frail
endeavour to apologise.

Later, though, drawn together by
a distaste for such 'untidy ends'
they agreed to meet again; whereupon
they giggled, reminisced, held hands
as though what they had made was love –
and not that happier outcome, friends.

Grandma

It was the midnight train; I was tired and edgy.
The advertisement portrayed – I wrote it down – a
'Skull-like young female, licking lips' and I added
'Prefer Grandma, even dead' as she newly was.
I walked home singing one of her Irish ballads.
Death is one thing, necrophilia another.

So I climbed up that ladder in the frescoed barn –
a soft ladder, swaying and collapsing under
my feet (my hands alone hauled me into the loft) –
and found, without surprise, a decomposed lady
who drew me down to her breast, with her disengaged
armbones, saying 'Come, my dearie, don't be afraid,
come to me' into a mess of sweetish decay.

It was a dream. I screamed and woke, put on the light,
dozed, woke again. For half a day I carried that
carcass in my own failing arms. Then remembered:
even the dead want to be loved for their own sake.
She was indeed my grandmother. She did not choose
to be dead and rotten. My blood too (Group A,
Rhesus negative, derived exactly from hers)
will suffer that deterioration; my much
modified version of her nose will fall away,
my longer bones collapse like hers. So let me now
apologise to my sons and their possible
children for the gruesomeness: we do not mean it.

Stewart Island

'But look at all this beauty'
said the hotel manager's wife
when asked how she could bear to
live there. True: there was a fine bay,
all hills and atmosphere; white
sand, and bush down to the sea's edge;
oyster-boats, too, and Maori
fishermen with Scottish names (she
ran off with one that autumn).
As for me, I walked on the beach;
it was too cold to swim. My
seven-year-old collected shells
and was bitten by sandflies;
my four-year-old paddled, until
a mad seagull jetted down
to jab its claws and beak into
his head. I had already
decided to leave the country.

Please Identify Yourself

British, more or less; Anglican, of a kind.
In Cookstown I dodge the less urgent question
when a friendly Ulsterbus driver raises it;
'You're not a Moneymore girl yourself?' he asks,
deadpan. I make a cowardly retrogression,
slip ten years back. 'No, I'm from New Zealand.'
'Are you now? Well, that's a coincidence:
the priest at Moneymore's a New Zealander.'
And there's the second question, unspoken,
Unanswered.
     I go to Moneymore
anonymously, and stare at all three churches.

In Belfast, though, where sides have to be taken,
I stop compromising – not that you'd guess,
seeing me hatless there among the hatted,
neutral voyeur among the shining faces
in the glossy Martyrs' Memorial Free Church.
The man himself is cheerleader in the pulpit
for crusader choruses: we're laved in blood,
marshalled in ranks. I chant the nursery tunes
and mentally cross myself. You can't stir me
with evangelistic hymns, Dr Paisley:
I know them. Nor with your computer-planned
sermon – Babylon, Revelation, whispers
of popery, slams at the IRA, more blood.
I scrawl incredulous notes under my hymnbook
and burn with Catholicism.

Later
hacking along the Lower Falls Road
against a gale, in my clerical black coat,
I meet a bright gust of tinselly children
in beads and lipstick and their mothers' dresses
for Hallowe'en; who chatter and surround me.

Over-reacting once again (a custom
of the country, not mine alone) I give them
all my loose change for their rattling tin
and my blessing – little enough. But now
to my tough Presbyterian ancestors,
Brooks and Hamilton, lying in the graves
I couldn't find at Moneymore and Cookstown
among so many unlabelled bones, I say:
I embrace you also, my dears.

Script

'Wet the tea, Jinny, the men are back:
I can hear them out there, talking, with the horses',
my mother's grandmother said. They both heard it,
she and her daughter – the wagon bumpily halted,
a rattle of harness, two familiar voices
in sentences to be identified later
and quoted endlessly. But the tea was cold
when the men came in. They'd been six miles away,
pausing to rest on Manurewa Hill
in a grove of trees – whence 'Fetch the nosebags, Dickie'
came clearly over. A freak wind, maybe:
soundwaves carrying, their words lifted up
and dropped on Drury. Eighty years ago,
long before the wireless was invented,
Grandma told us. It made a good story:
baffling. But then, so was the real thing –
radio.
        My father understood it.
Out on the bush farm at Te Rau a Moa
as a teenager he patiently constructed
little fiddly devices, sat for hours
every day adjusting a cat's whisker,
filtering morse through headphones. Later came
loudspeakers, and the whole family could gather
to hear the creaky music of 1YA.
So my father's people were technicians, is that it?
And my mother's were communicators, yes? –
Who worked as a barber in the evenings
for the talking's sake? Who became a teacher –
and who was in love with tractors? No prizes.
Don't classify. Leave the air-waves open.

We each extract what we most need. My sons
rig out their rooms with stereo equipment.
I walk dozily through the house
in the mornings with a neat black box,
audible newspaper, timekeeper and -saver,
sufficient for days like that.
                                    On days like this
I sit in my own high borrowed grove
and let the leafy air clear my mind
for reception. The slow pigeon-flight,
the scraped-wire pipping of some bird,
the loamy scent, offer themselves to me
as little presents, part of an exchange
to be continued and continually
(is this a rondo? that professor asked)
perpetuated. It is not like music,
though the effects can strike as music does:
it is more like agriculture, a nourishing
of the growth-mechanisms, a taking-in
of food for what will flower and seed and sprout.

On a path in the wood two white-haired women
are marching arm in arm, singing a hymn.
A girl stops me to ask where I bought my sandals.
I say 'In Italy, I think' and we laugh.
I am astonished several times a day.
When I get home I shall make tea or coffee
for whoever is there, talk and listen to talk,
share food and living-space. There will always
be time to reassemble the frail components
of this afternoon, to winnow the scattered sounds
dropped into my range, and rescue from them
a seed-hoard for transmission. There will be
always the taking-in and the sending-out.

Things

There are worse things than having behaved foolishly in
  public.
There are worse things than these miniature betrayals,
committed or endured or suspected; there are worse
  things
than not being able to sleep for thinking about them.
It is 5 a.m. All the worse things come stalking in
and stand icily about the bed looking worse and worse
                                    and worse.

Prelude

Is it the long dry grass that is so erotic,
waving about us with hair-fine fronds of straw,
with feathery flourishes of seed, inviting us
to cling together, fall, roll into it
blind and gasping, smothered by stalks and hair,
pollen and each other's tongues on our hot faces?
Then imagine if the summer rain were to come,
heavy drops hissing through the warm air,
a sluice on our wet bodies, plastering us
with strands of delicious grass; a hum in our ears.

We walk a yard apart, talking
of literature and of botany.
We have known each other, remotely, for nineteen years.

Accidental

We awakened facing each other
across the white counterpane.
I prefer to be alone in the mornings.
The waiter offered us
melon, papaya, orange juice or fresh raspberries.
We did not discuss it.

All those years of looking but not touching:
at most a kiss in a taxi.
And now this accident,
this blind unstoppable robot walk
into a conspiracy of our bodies.
Had we ruined the whole thing?

The waiter waited:
it was his business to appear composed.
Perhaps we should make it ours also?
We moved an inch or two closer together.
Our toes touched. We looked. We had decided.
Papaya then; and coffee and rolls. Of course.

A Walk in the Snow

Neighbours lent her a tall feathery dog
to make her expedition seem natural.
She couldn't really fancy a walk alone,
drawn though she was to the shawled whiteness,
the flung drifts of wool. She was not a walker.
Her winter pleasures were in firelit rooms –
entertaining friends with inventive dishes
or with sherry, conversation, palm-reading:
'You've suffered' she'd say. 'Of course, life is suffering . . .'
holding a wrist with her little puffy hand
older than her face. She was writing a novel.
But today there was the common smothered in snow,
blanked-out, white as meringue, the paths gone:
a few mounds of bracken spikily veiled
and the rest smooth succulence. They pocked it,
she and the dog; they wrote on it with their feet –
her suede boots, his bright flurrying paws.
It was their snow, and they took it.
                                   That evening
the poltergeist, the switcher-on of lights
and conjuror with ashtrays, was absent.
The house lay mute. She hesitated a moment
at bedtime before the Valium bottle;
then, to be on the safe side, took her usual;
and swam into a deep snowy sleep
where a lodge (was it?) and men in fur hats,
and the galloping . . . and something about . . .

House-talk

Through my pillow, through mattress, carpet, floor and
   ceiling,
sounds ooze up from the room below:
footsteps, chinking crockery, hot-water pipes groaning,
the muffled clunk of the refrigerator door,
and voices. They are trying to be quiet,
my son and his friends, home late in the evening.

Tones come softly filtered through the layers of padding.
I hear the words but not what the words are,
as on my radio when the batteries are fading.
Voices are reduced to a muted music:
Andrew's bass, his friend's tenor, the indistinguishable
light murmurs of the girls; occasional giggling.

Surely wood and plaster retain something
in their grain of all the essences they absorb?
This house has been lived in for ninety years,
nine by us. It has heard all manner of talking.
Its porous fabric must be saturated
with words. I offer it my peaceful breathing.

Instead of an Interview

The hills, I told them; and water, and the clear air
(not yielding to more journalistic probings);
and a river or two, I could say, and certain bays
and ah, those various and incredible hills . . .

And all my family still in the one city
within walking distances of each other
through streets I could follow blind. My school was gone
and half my Thorndon smashed for the motorway
but every corner revealed familiar settings
for the dreams I'd not bothered to remember –
ingrained; ingrown; incestuous: like the country.

And another city offering me a lover
and quite enough friends to be going on with;
bookshops; galleries; gardens; fish in the sea;
lemons and passionfruit growing free as the bush.
Then the bush itself; and the wild grand south;
and wooden houses in occasional special towns.

And not a town or a city I could live in.
Home, as I explained to a weeping niece,
home is London; and England, Ireland, Europe.
I have come home with a suitcase full of stones –
of shells and pebbles, pottery, pieces of bark:
here they lie around the floor of my study
as I telephone a cable 'Safely home'

and moments later, thinking of my dears,
wish the over-resonant word cancelled:
'Arrived safely' would have been clear enough,
neutral, kinder. But another loaded word
creeps up now to interrogate me.
By going back to look, after thirteen years,
have I made myself for the first time an exile?

Crab

Late at night we wrench open a crab;
flesh bursts out of its cup

in pastel colours. The dark fronds attract me:
Poison, you say, Dead Men's Fingers –

don't put them in your mouth, stop!
They brush over my tongue, limp and mossy,

until you snatch them from me, as you snatch
yourself, gently, if I come too close.

Here are the permitted parts of the crab,
wholesome on their nests of lettuce

and we are safe again in words.
All day the kitchen will smell of sea.

Blue Glass

The underworld of children becomes the overworld
when Janey or Sharon shuts the attic door
on a sunny afternoon and tiptoes in sandals
that softly waffle-print the dusty floor

to the cluttered bed below the skylight,
managing not to sneeze as she lifts
newspapers, boxes, gap-stringed tennis-racquets
and a hamster's cage to the floor, and shifts

the tasselled cover to make a clean surface
and a pillow to be tidy under her head
before she straightens, mouths the dark sentence,
and lays herself out like a mummy on the bed.

Her wrists are crossed. The pads of her fingertips
trace the cold glass emblem where it lies
like a chain of hailstones melting in the dips
above her collarbones. She needs no eyes

to see it: the blue bead necklace, of sapphire
or lapis, or of other words she knows
which might mean blueness: amethyst, azure,
chalcedony can hardly say how it glows.

She stole it. She tells herself that she found it.
It's hers now. It owns her. She slithers among
its globular teeth, skidding on blue pellets.
Ice-beads flare and blossom on her tongue,

turn into flowers, populate the spaces
around and below her. The attic has become
her bluebell wood. Among their sappy grasses
the light-fringed gas-flames of bluebells hum.

They lift her body like a cloud of petals.
High now, floating, this is what she sees:
granular bark six inches from her eyeballs;
the wood of rafters is the wood of trees.

Her breathing moistens the branches' undersides;
the sunlight in an interrupted shaft
warms her legs and lulls her as she rides
on air, a slender and impossible raft

of bones and flesh; and whether it is knowledge
or a limpid innocence on which she feeds
for power hasn't mattered. She turns the necklace
kindly in her fingers, and soothes the beads.

Toads

Let's be clear about this: I love toads.

So when I found our old one dying,
washed into the drain by flood-water
in the night and then – if I can bring myself
to say it – scalded by soapy lather
I myself had let out of the sink,
we suffered it through together.

It was the summer of my father's death.
I saw his spirit in every visiting creature,
in every small thing at risk of harm:
bird, moth, butterfly, beetle,
the black rabbit lolloping along concrete,
lost in suburbia; and our toad.

If we'd seen it once a year that was often,
but the honour of being chosen by it
puffed us up: a toad of our own
trusting us not to hurt it
when we had to lift it out of its den
to let the plumber get at the water-main.

And now this desperate damage: the squat
compactness unhinged, made powerless.
Dark, straight, its legs extended,
flippers paralysed, it lay lengthwise
flabby-skinned across my palm,
cold and stiff as the Devil's penis.

I laid it on soil; the shoulders managed
a few slow twitches, pulled it an inch forward.
But the blowflies knew: they called it dead
and stippled its back with rays of pearly stitching.
Into the leaves with it then, poor toad,
somewhere cool, where I can't watch it.

Perhaps it was very old? Perhaps it was ready?
Small comfort, through ten guilt-ridden days.
And then, one moist midnight, out in the country,
a little shadow shaped like a brown leaf
hopped out of greener leaves and came to me.
Twice I had to lift it from my doorway:

a gently throbbing handful – calm, comely,
its feet tickling my palm like soft bees.

Creosote

What is it, what is it? Quick: that whiff,
that black smell – black that's really brown,
sharp that's really oily and yet rough,

a tang of splinters burning the tongue,
almost as drunkening as hot tar
or cowshit, a wonderful ringing pong.

It's fence-posts, timber yards, the woodshed;
it bundles you into the Baby Austin
and rushes you back to early childhood.

It's Uncle's farm; it's the outside dunny;
it's flies and heat; or it's boats and rope
and that salt-cracked slipway down from the jetty.

It's brushes oozing with sloshy stain;
it's a tin at the back of the shed: open it,
snort it! You can't: the lid's stuck on.

U. A. Fanthorpe

The List

Flawlessly typed, and spaced
At the proper intervals,
Serene and lordly, they pace
Along tomorrow's list
Like giftbearers on a frieze.

In tranquil order, arrayed
With the basic human equipment –
A name, a time, a number –
They advance on the future.

Not more harmonious who pace
Holding a hawk, a fish, a jar
(The customary offerings)
Along the Valley of the Kings.

Tomorrow these names will turn nasty,
Senile, pregnant, late,
Handicapped, handcuffed, unhandy,
Muddled, moribund, mute,

Be stained by living. But here,
Orderly, equal, right,
On the edge of tomorrow, they pause
Like giftbearers on a frieze

With the proper offering,
A time, a number, a name.
I am the artist, the typist;
I did my best for them.

Stanton Drew

First you dismantle the landscape.
Take away everything you first
Thought of. Trees must go,
Roads, of course, the church,
Houses, hedges, livestock, a wire
Fence. The river can stay,
But loses its stubby fringe
Of willows. What do you
See now? Grass, the circling
Mendip rim, with its notches
Fresh, like carving. A sky
Like ours, but empty along
Its lower levels. And earth
Stripped of its future, tilted
Into meaning by these stones,
Pitted and unemphatic. Re-create them.
They are the most permanent
Presences here, but cattle, weather,
Archaeologists have rubbed against them.
Still in season they will
Hold the winter sun poised
Over Maes Knoll's white cheek,
Chain the moon's footsteps to
The pattern of their dance.
Stand inside the circle. Put
Your hand on stone. Listen
To the past's long pulse.

Casehistory: Alison (head injury)

(She looks at her photograph)

I would like to have known
My husband's wife, my mother's only daughter.
A bright girl she was.

Enmeshed in comforting
Fat, I wonder at her delicate angles.
Her autocratic knee

Like a Degas dancer's
Adjusts to the observer with airy poise,
That now lugs me upstairs

Hardly. Her face, broken
By nothing sharper than smiles, holds in its smiles
What I have forgotten.

She knows my father's dead,
And grieves for it, and smiles. She has digested
Mourning. Her smile shows it.

I, who need reminding
Every morning, shall never get over what
I do not remember.

Consistency matters.
I should like to keep faith with her lack of faith,
But forget her reasons.

Proud of this younger self,
I assert her achievements, her A levels,
Her job with a future.

Poor clever girl! I know,
For all my damaged brain, something she doesn't:
I am her future.

A bright girl she was.

Earthed

Not precisely, like a pylon or
A pop-up toaster, but in a general
Way, stuck in the mud.

Not budding out of it like gipsies,
Laundry lashed to a signpost, dieting on
Nettles and hedgehogs,

Not lodged in its layers like badgers,
Tuned to the runes of its home-made walls, wearing
Its shape like a skin,

Not even securely rooted, like
Tribesmen tied to the same allotment, sure of
The local buses,

But earthed for all that, in the chalky
Kent mud, thin sharp ridges between wheel-tracks, in
Surrey's wild gravel,

In serious Cotswold uplands, where
Limestone confines the verges like yellow teeth,
And trees look sideways.

Everything from the clouds downwards holds
Me in its web, like the local newspapers,
Routinely special,

Or Somerset belfries, so highly
Parochial that Gloucestershire has none, or
Literate thrushes,

Conscientiously practising the
Phrases Browning liked, the attitude Hughes noticed,
Or supermarkets

Where the cashiers' rudeness is native
To the district, though the bread's not, or gardens,
Loved more than children,

Bright with resourcefulness and smelling
Of rain. This narrow island charged with echoes
And whispers snares me.

Not My Best Side

(*Uccello*: St George and the Dragon, *The National Gallery*)

I

Not my best side, I'm afraid.
The artist didn't give me a chance to
Pose properly, and as you can see,
Poor chap, he had this obsession with
Triangles, so he left off two of my
Feet. I didn't comment at the time
(What, after all, are two feet
To a monster?) but afterwards
I was sorry for the bad publicity.
Why, I said to myself, should my conqueror
Be so ostentatiously beardless, and ride
A horse with a deformed neck and square hoofs?
Why should my victim be so
Unattractive as to be inedible,
And why should she have me literally
On a string? I don't mind dying
Ritually, since I always rise again,
But I should have liked a little more blood
To show they were taking me seriously.

II

It's hard for a girl to be sure if
She wants to be rescued. I mean, I quite
Took to the dragon. It's nice to be
Liked, if you know what I mean. He was
So nicely physical, with his claws
And lovely green skin, and that sexy tail,
And the way he looked at me,

33

He made me feel he was all ready to
Eat me. And any girl enjoys that.
So when this boy turned up, wearing machinery,
On a really *dangerous* horse, to be honest,
I didn't much fancy him. I mean,
What was he like underneath the hardware?
He might have acne, blackheads or even
Bad breath for all I could tell, but the dragon –
Well, you could see all his equipment
At a glance. Still, what could I do?
The dragon got himself beaten by the boy,
And a girl's got to think of her future.

III

I have diplomas in Dragon
Management and Virgin Reclamation.
My horse is the latest model, with
Automatic transmission and built-in
Obsolescence. My spear is custom-built,
And my prototype armour
Still on the secret list. You can't
Do better than me at the moment.
I'm qualified and equipped to the
Eyebrow. So why be difficult?
Don't you want to be killed and/or rescued
In the most contemporary way? Don't
You want to carry out the roles
That sociology and myth have designed for you?
Don't you realise that, by being choosy,
You are endangering job-prospects
In the spear- and horse-building industries?
What, in any case, does it matter what
You want? You're in my way.

Horticultural Show

These are Persephone's fruits
Of the underyear. These will guide us
Through the slow dream of winter.

Onions her paleskinned lamps.
Rub them for strange knowledge. They shine
With the light of the tomb.

Drawn in fine runes along
Hard green rinds, the incomprehensible
Initiation of the marrow.

All orange energy driven
Down to a final hair, these carrots
Have been at the heart of darkness.

And parti-coloured leeks,
Their green hair plaited, like Iroquois braves,
Leaning exhausted in corners.

Holystoned the presence
Of potatoes, pure white and stained pink.
Persephone's bread.

Sacrificed beetroots
Display their bleeding hearts. We read
The future in these entrails.

Out in the world excitable
Ponies caper, Punch batters Judy, a man
Creates a drystone wall in thirty minutes,

Arrows fly, coconuts fall, crocodiles
And Jubilee mugs, disguised as children,
Cope with candyfloss, the band
Adds its slow waltz heart beat.

Here in the tent, in the sepia hush,
Persephone's fruits utter where they have been,
Where we are going.

The Contributors

Not your fault, gentlemen.
We acquit you of the calculatedly
Equivalent gift, the tinsel token.
Mary, maybe, fancied something more practical:
A layette, or at least a premium bond.
Firmly you gave the extravagantly
Useless, your present the unwrapped
Hard-edged stigma of vocation.

Not your fault, beasts,
Who donated your helpless animal
Rectitude to the occasion.
Not yours the message of the goblin
Robin, the red-nosed reindeer,
Nor had you in mind the yearly
Massacre of the poultry innocent,
Whom we judge correct for the feast.

Not your fault, Virgin,
Muddling along in the manger,
With your confused old man,
Your bastard baby, in conditions
No social worker could possibly approve.
How could your improvised, improvident
Holiness predict our unholy family Xmas,
Our lonely overdoses, deepfrozen bonhomie?

Stations Underground

1   Fanfare

(*for Winifrid Fanthorpe, born 5 February 1895, died 13 November 1978*)

You, in the old photographs, are always
The one with the melancholy half-smile, the one
Who couldn't quite relax into the joke.

My extrovert dog of a father,
With his ragtime blazer and his swimming togs
Tucked like a swiss roll under his arm,
Strides in his youth towards us down some esplanade,

Happy as Larry. You, on his other arm,
Are anxious about the weather forecast,
His overdraft, or early closing day.

You were good at predicting failure: marriages
Turned out wrong because you said they would.
You knew the rotations of armistice and war,
Watched politicians' fates with gloomy approval.

All your life you lived in a minefield,
And were pleased, in a quiet way, when mines
Exploded. You never actually said
I told you so, but we could tell you meant it.

Crisis was your element. You kept your funny stories,
Your music-hall songs for doodlebug and blitz-nights.
In the next cubicle, after a car-crash, I heard you
Amusing the nurses with your trench wit through the blood.

Magic alerted you. Green, knives and ladders
Will always scare me through your tabus.
Your nightmare was Christmas; so much organised
Compulsory whoopee to be got through.

You always had some stratagem for making
Happiness keep its distance. Disaster
Was what you planned for. You always
Had hoarded loaves or candles up your sleeve.

Houses crumbled around your ears, taps leaked,
Electric light bulbs went out all over England,
Because for you homes were only provisional,
Bivouacs on the stony mountain of living.

You were best at friendship with chars, gipsies,
Or very far-off foreigners. Well-meaning neighbours
Were dangerous because they lived near.

Me too you managed best at a distance. On the landline
From your dugout to mine, your nightly
Pass, friend was really often quite jovial.

You were the lonely figure in the doorway
Waving goodbye in the cold, going back to a sink-full
Of crockery dirtied by those you loved. We
Left you behind to deal with our crusts and gristle.

I know why you chose now to die. You foresaw
Us approaching the Delectable Mountains,
And didn't feel up to all the cheers and mafficking.

But how, dearest, will even you retain your
Special brand of hard-bitten stoicism
Among the halleluyas of the triumphant dead?

2 Four Dogs

1 CERBERUS

The first was known simply
As *the dog*. Later writers gave him a name,
Three heads, a collar of serpents,
And a weakness for cake.
They also claimed he could be
Calmed by magic, charmed by music,
And even, on one occasion, thrashed.

Later writers can seldom be trusted.
Primary sources are more reliable:
This dog guarded his master's gate,
Wagged his ears and tail at visitors,
Admitted them all, and saw to it
That nobody ever got out.

2 ANUBIS

The civil Egyptians made
Their dog half man. The dog end
Had the usual doggy tastes
For digging, and bones. But the human half
Was drawn to conservation and chemistry,
Liked pickling, preserving, dissecting,
Distillation; added artistry
To the dog's enthusiasm. Undertaking
Became Egyptian art.

3 EL PERRO (GOYA)

There was a man who never blinked.
Helmeted in deafness, he set down
What he saw: the unembarrassed beastliness
Of humanity, country picnics, rape,
Blank-faced politicians, idiot obstinate kings,
Famine, firing-squads, milkmaids.
He charted nightmare's dominion
On his house's walls. To him appeared
The thing itself, snouting its way
Up from underground. He drew it
As it was: darkness, a dog's head,
Mild, mongrel, appalling.

4 SHANDY

The fourth dog lives in my house with me
Like a sister, loves me doggedly,
Guiltily, abstractedly; disobeys me
When I am not looking. I love her
Abstractedly, guiltily; feed her; try
Not to let her know she reminds me
Of the other dogs.

3   At the Ferry

Laconic as anglers and, like them, submissive,
The grey-faced loiterers on the bank,
Charon, of your river.

They are waiting their turn. Nothing we do
Distracts them much. It was you, Charon, I saw,
Refracted in a woman's eyes.

Patient, she sat in a wheelchair,
In an X-ray department, waiting for someone
To do something to her,

Given a magazine, folded back
At the problem page: *What should I do*
About my husband's impotence?

Is a registry office marriage
Second-best? I suffer from a worrying
Discharge from my vagina.

In her hands she held the thing obediently;
Obediently moved her eyes in the direction
Of the problems of the restless living.

But her mind deferred to another dimension.
Outward bound, tenderly inattentive, she was waiting,
Charon, for you.

And the nineteen-stone strong man, felled
By his spawning brain, lying still to the sound
Of the DJ's brisk chirrup;

He wasn't listening, either. He was on the lookout
For the flurry of water as your craft
Comes about in the current.

I saw you once, boatman, lean by your punt-pole
On an Oxford river, in the dubious light
Between willow and water,

Where I had been young and lonely, being
Now loved, and older, saw you in the tender, reflective
Gaze of the living

Looking down at me, deliberate,
And strange in the half-light, saying nothing,
Claiming me, Charon, for life.

7 The Passing of Alfred

'He [Tennyson] died with his hand on his Shakespeare, and the
moon shining full into the window over him . . . A worthy end.'

Queen Victoria, *Journal*

Our fathers were good at dying.
They did it lingeringly,
As if they liked it; correctly,
With earnest attention to detail,
Codicils brought up to date,
Forgiveness, confession, last-gasp
Penitence properly witnessed
By responsible persons. Attorneys,
Clerics, physicians, all knew their place
In the civil pavane of dying.

Households discharged
Their methodical duties: said farewell
In order of precedence, outdoor staff first,
Faithful hounds respectfully mourning,
Lastly the widow-to-be, already
Pondering a transformed wardrobe.

They died in the houses,
The beds they were born in,
They died where they lived, between
Known sheets, to the obbligato
Of familiar creaks and ticks.

We who differ, whose dears are absorbed
Into breezy wards for routine terminations,
Envy our fathers their decorous endings
In error. Nothing makes extinction easy.
They also died appallingly, over
The family breakfast-cups; bloodily
In childbed; graveyard coughed themselves
Into coffins; declined from heart-break
And hunger. And however resigned,
Orderly, chaste, aesthetic the passing of Alfred,
Remorse, regret still shadowed the living after.

Like us they ran from habit to tell good news
To dead ears; like us they dreamed
Of childhood, and being forgiven;
And the dead followed them, as they do us,
Tenderly through darkness,
But fade when we turn to look in the upper air.

Half-term

Always autumn, in my memory.
Butter ringing the drilled teashop crumpets;
Handmade chocolates, rich enough to choke you,
Brought in special smooth paper from Town.

(Back at school, the square tall piles
Of bread, featureless red jam in basins,
Grace, a shuffle of chairs, the separate table
For the visiting lacrosse team.)

Long awkward afternoons in hotel lounges,
Islanded in swollen armchairs, eyeing
Aristocratic horses in irrelevant magazines.
Should I be talking to Them?

(Back at school the raptly selfish
Snatch at self: the clashing
Determined duets in cold practising-
Rooms, the passionate solitary knitting.)

Inadequacies of presentation, perceived
By parents' temporary friends; hair, manners,
Clothes, have failed to adjust.
I don't know the rules of snooker.

(Back at school, the stiff reliable
Awkwardnesses of work. History test
On Monday morning. Deponent verbs.
I have never been good at maths.)

Saying goodbye. There are tears
And hugs, relief, regret. They,
Like me, return to a patterned life
Whose rules are easy. Unworthily

I shall miss chocolate, crumpets,
Comfort, but not the love I only
Sense as they go, waving to the end,
Vague in the streetlamps of November.

(Back at school the bullies,
Tyrants and lunatics are waiting.
I can deal with them.)

Hang-gliders in January

(for C. K.)

Like all miracles, it has a rational
Explanation; and like all miracles, insists
On being miraculous. We toiled
In the old car up from the lacklustre valley,
Taking the dogs because somebody had to,
At the heel of a winter Sunday afternoon

Into a sky of shapes flying:
Pot-bellied, shipless sails, dragonflies towering
Still with motion, daytime enormous bats,
Titanic tropical fish, and men,
When we looked, men strapped to wings,
Men wearing wings, men flying

Over a landscape too emphatic
To be understood: humdrum fields
With hedges and grass, the mythical river,
Beyond it the forest, the foreign high country.
The exact sun, navigating downwards
To end the revels, and you, and me,
The dogs, even, enjoying a scamper,
Avoiding scuffles.

It was all quite simple, really. We saw
The aground flyers, their casques and belts
And defenceless legs; we saw the earthed wings
Being folded like towels; we saw
The sheepskin-coated wives and mothers
Loyally watching; we saw a known,
Explored landscape by sunset-light,

We saw for ourselves how it was done,
From takeoff to landing. But nothing cancelled
The cipher of the soaring, crucified men,
Which we couldn't unravel; which gave us
Also, somehow, the freedom of air. Not
In vast caravels, triumphs of engineering,
But as men always wanted, simply,
Like a bird at home in the sky.

Father in the Railway Buffet

What are you doing here, ghost, among these urns,
These film-wrapped sandwiches and help-yourself
   biscuits,
Upright and grand, with your stick, hat and gloves,
Your breath of eau-de-cologne?

What have you to say to these head-scarfed tea-ladies,
For whom your expensive vowels are exotic as Japan?
Stay, ghost, in your proper haunts, the clubland
   smokerooms,
Where you know the waiters by name.

You have no place among these damp and nameless.
Why do you walk here? *I came to say goodbye.*
You were ashamed of me for being different.
It didn't matter.

You who never even learned to queue?

Growing Up

I wasn't good
At being a baby. Burrowed my way
Through the long yawn of infancy,
Masking by instinct how much I knew
Of the senior world, sabotaging
As far as I could, biding my time,
Biting my rattle, my brother (in private),
Shoplifting daintily into my pram.
Not a good baby,
No.

I wasn't good
At being a child. I missed
The innocent age. Children,
Being childish, were beneath me.
Adults I despised or distrusted. They
Would label my every disclosure
Precocious, *naive*, whatever it was.
I disdained definition, preferred to be surly.
Not a nice child,
No.

I wasn't good
At adolescence. There was a dance,
A catchy rhythm; I was out of step.
My body capered, nudging me
With hairy, fleshy growths and monthly outbursts,
To join the party. I tried to annul
The future, pretended I knew it already,
Was caught bloody-thighed, a criminal

Guilty of puberty.
Not a nice girl,
No.

(My hero, intransigent Emily,
Cauterised her own-dog-mauled
Arm with a poker,
Struggled to die on her feet,
Never told anyone anything.)

I wasn't good
At growing up. Never learned
The natives' art of life. Conversation
Disintegrated as I touched it,
So I played mute, wormed along years,
Reciting the hard-learned arcane litany
Of cliché, my company passport.
Not a nice person,
No.

The gift remains
Masonic, dark. But age affords
A vocation even for wallflowers.
Called to be connoisseur, I collect,
Admire, the effortless bravura
Of other people's lives, proper and comely,
Treading the measure, shopping, chaffing,
Quarrelling, drinking, not knowing
How right they are, or how, like well-oiled bolts,
Swiftly and sweet, they slot into the grooves
Their ancestors smoothed out along the grain.

Dig

The place: once Troy; the characters:
Ghosts of two Trojan lovers who lived there;

The time: a dream of mine; the plot:
Nothing . . . driftings and strayings round a spot

That neither recognised. Where were
The god-built walls, the gates, the bright river?

A wind got up: the famous wind.
The sad ghosts sighed and drifted like dry sand.

Only an archaeologist
Could disinter what these cold phantoms missed:

Village on top of village; town
On town; city on city; Trojan ground

Lay aeons under Hissarlik.
Schliemann alone could recognise the wreck

And spell it Ilium; he who
Unpicked the wayward river's fluent clew,

Found the old bed of Scamander
Far from Mendere's prosy meander.

My dream-ghosts never traced their Troy.
In waking life, dear lost one, you and I

Whose Troy fell centuries ago
Find, when we meet, the malign debris grow:

Misunderstandings; blunders; slips;
Faults; different lives that have developed since.

Useless to salvage what has been.
At once the monstrous midden sprouts between.

The Person's Tale

'In consequence of a slight indisposition, an anodyne had been
prescribed, from the effects of which [the author] fell asleep . . .
On awaking . . [he] eagerly wrote down the lines that are here
preserved. At this moment he was unfortunately called out by a
person on business from Porlock, and detained by him above an
hour . . .'

S. T. C.

That the Muses have no more fervent
Devotee than myself may not be generally
Known outside Porlock. As a man of the cloth
I am, I trust, superior to mere vulgar
Appetite for fame. 'Full many a gem
Of purest ray serene . . .' I am, I hope, resigned
To being such a gem; an unseen blush.
But to allow myself to be presented
By Mr C— to posterity as a *person*
Goes beyond the limits of even clerical
Diffidence. It was, I may say, in pursuit

Of my pastoral duties that I made
The not inconsiderable journey from my parsonage
To the farmhouse, at Mr C —'s own
Most vehement behest. Prepared for any
Extreme office, I presented myself
Before Mr C—, *Sir*, said I, *I am here.*
The very man, quoth he, clasping me in
A distasteful embrace. *Most reverend sir –*
Then for two hours detained me at his door
With chronicles of colic, stomach, bowels,
Of nightly sweats, the nightmare, cramps, diarrhoea
(Your pardon, Delicacy! Merely the word appals),
All the while straining me to his bosom, like
His own deplorable Mariner, neglected hygiene
Rendering contiguity less than welcome,
The more as I infallibly discerned
The less pleasing features of addiction
To the poppy, prescribed, he affirmed,
As anodyne against the dysentery.
And now, it seems, I am the guilty *person*
Who cut off inspiration in its prime.
Quite otherwise. Myself had on the way
Entertained the notion of an Acrostick, a form
Of harmless mirth whereby I have achieved
Some slender fame among the Porlock fair.
Alas! the frail thing could not survive
Two hours of Mr C —'s internal ills.
I am the loser, first of my Acrostick,
Then of my character, for surely *person*
Denotes nonentity, a man of straw –
And the proud name of Porlock sullied too!

Tony Harrison

Durham

'St Cuthbert's shrine,
founded 999'
       (mnemonic)

ANARCHY and GROW YOUR OWN
whitewashed on to crumbling stone
fade in the drizzle. There's a man
handcuffed to warders in a black sedan.
A butcher dumps a sodden sack
of sheep pelts off his bloodied back,
then hangs the morning's killings out,
cup-cum-muzzle on each snout.

I've watched where this 'distinguished see'
takes off into infinity,
among transistor antennae,
and student smokers getting high,
and visiting Norwegian choirs
in raptures over Durham's spires,
lifers, rapists, thieves, ant-size
circle and circle at their exercise.

And Quasimodo's bird's-eye view
of big wigs and their retinue,
a five car Rolls Royce motorcade
of judgement draped in Town Hall braid,
I've watched the golden maces sweep
from courtrooms to the Castle keep
through winding Durham, the elect
before whom ids must genuflect.

But some stay standing and at one
God's irritating carrillon
brings you to me; I feel like the hunch-
back taking you for lunch;
then bed. All afternoon two church-
high prison helicopters search
for escapees down by the Wear
and seem as though they're coming here.

Listen! Their choppers guillotine
all the enemies there've ever been
of Church and State, including me
for taking this small liberty.
Liberal, lover, communist,
Czechoslovakia, Cuba, grist,
grist for the power-driven mill
weltering in overkill.

And England? Quiet Durham? Threat
smokes off our lives like steam off wet
subsidences when summer rain
drenches the workings. You complain
that the machinery of sudden death,
Fascism, the hot bad breath
of Powers down small countries' necks
shouldn't interfere with sex.

They *are* sex, love, we must include
all these in love's beatitude.
Bad weather and the public mess
drive us to private tenderness,
though I wonder if together we,
alone two hours, can ever be

love's anti-bodies in the sick,
sick body politic.

At best we're medieval masons, skilled
but anonymous within our guild,
at worst defendants hooded in a car
charged with something sinister.
On the *status quo*'s huge edifice
we're just excrescences that kiss,
cathedral gargoyles that obtrude
their acts of 'moral turpitude'.

But turpitude still keeps me warm
in foul weather as I head for home
down New Elvet, through the town,
past the butcher closing down,
hearing the belfry jumble time
out over Durham. As I climb
rain blankets the pithills, mist
the chalkings of the anarchist.

I wait for the six-five Plymouth train
glowering at Durham. First rain,
then hail, like teeth spit from a skull,
then fog obliterate it. As we pull
out of the station through the dusk and fog,
there, lighting up, is Durham, dog
chasing its own cropped tail,
University, Cathedral, Gaol.

National Trust

Bottomless pits. There's one in Castleton,
and stout upholders of our law and order
one day thought its depth worth wagering on
and borrowed a convict hush-hush from his warder
and winched him down; and back, flayed, grey, mad,
   dumb.

Not even a good flogging made him holler!

O gentlemen, a better way to plumb
the depths of Britain's dangling a scholar,
say, here at the booming shaft at Towanroath,
now National Trust, a place where they got tin,
those gentlemen who silenced the men's oath
and killed the language that they swore it in.

The dumb go down in history and disappear
and not one gentleman 's been brought to book:

Mes den hep tavas a-gollas y dyr

(Cornish) –
               'the tongueless man gets his land took.'

Them & [uz]

for Professors Richard Hoggart & Leon Cortez

I

αιαῖ, ay, ay! . . . stutterer Demosthenes
gob full of pebbles outshouting seas –

4 words only of *mi 'art aches* and . . . 'Mine's broken,
you barbarian, T.W.!' *He* was nicely spoken.
'Can't have our glorious heritage done to death!'

I played the Drunken Porter in *Macbeth*.

'Poetry's the speech of kings. You're one of those
Shakespeare gives the comic bits to: prose!
All poetry (even Cockney Keats?) you see
's been dubbed by [Λs] into RP,
Received Pronunciation, please believe [Λs]
your speech is in the hands of the Receivers.'

'We say [Λs] not [uz], T.W.!' That shut my trap.
I doffed my flat a's (as in 'flat cap')
my mouth all stuffed with glottals, great
lumps to hawk up and spit out . . . *E-nun-ci-ate*!

II

So right, yer buggers, then! We'll occupy
your lousy leasehold Poetry.

I chewed up Littererchewer and spat the bones
into the lap of dozing Daniel Jones,
dropped the initials I'd been harried as
and used my *name* and own voice: [uz] [uz] [uz],
ended sentences with by, with, from,
and spoke the language that I spoke at home.
RIP RP, RIP T.W.
I'm *Tony* Harrison no longer you!

You can tell the Receivers where to go
(and not aspirate it) once you know
Wordsworth's *matter/water* are full rhymes,
[uz] can be loving as well as funny.

My first mention in the *Times*
automatically made Tony Anthony!

Long Distance

I

Your bed's got two wrong sides. Your life's all grouse.
I let your phone-call take its dismal course:

Ah can't stand it no more, this empty house!

Carrots choke us wi'out your mam's white sauce!

Them sweets you brought me, you can have 'em back.
Ah'm diabetic now. Got all the facts.
(The diabetes comes hard on the track
of two coronaries and cataracts.)

Ah've allus liked things sweet! But now ah push
food down mi throat! Ah'd sooner do wi'out.
And t'only reason now for beer 's to flush
(so t'dietician said) mi kidneys out.

When I come round, they'll be laid out, the sweets,
Lifesavers, my father's New World treats,
still in the big brown bag, and only bought
rushing through JFK as a last thought.

II

Though my mother was already two years dead
Dad kept her slippers warming by the gas,
put hot water bottles her side of the bed
and still went to renew her transport pass.

You couldn't just drop in. You had to phone.
He'd put you off an hour to give him time
to clear away her things and look alone
as though his still raw love were such a crime.

He couldn't risk my blight of disbelief
though sure that very soon he'd hear her key
scrape in the rusted lock and end his grief.
He *knew* she'd just popped out to get the tea.

I believe life ends with death, and that is all.
You haven't both gone shopping; just the same,
in my new black leather phone book there's your name
and the disconnected number I still call.

Working

Among stooped getters, grimy, knacker-bare,
head down thrusting a 3 cwt corf
turned your crown bald, your golden hair
chafed fluffy first and then scuffed off,
chick's back, then eggshell, that sunless white.
You strike sparks and plenty but can't see.
You've been underneath too long to stand the light.
You're lost in this sonnet for the bourgeoisie.

Patience Kershaw, bald hurryer, fourteen,
this wordshift and inwit's a load of crap
for dumping on a slagheap, I mean
th'art nobbut summat as wants raking up.

I stare into the fire. Your skinned skull shines.
I close my eyes. That makes a dark like mines.

Wherever hardship held its tongue the job
's breaking the silence of the worked-out-gob.

Flood

His home address was inked inside his cap
and on every piece of paper that he carried
even across the church porch of the snap
that showed him with mi mam just minutes married.

But if ah'm found at 'ome (he meant found dead)
turn t'water off. Through his last years he nursed,
more than a fear of dying, a deep dread
of his last bath running over, or a burst.

Each night towards the end he'd pull the flush
then wash, then in pyjamas, rain or snow,
go outside, kneel down in the yard, and push
the stopcock as far off as it would go.

For though hoping that he'd drop off in his sleep
he was most afraid, I think, of not being 'found'
there in their house, his ark, on firm Leeds ground
but somewhere that kept moving, cold, dark, deep.

Tugging my forelock fathoming Xenophon
grimed Greek exams with grease and lost me marks,
so I whisper when the barber asks *Owt on?*
No, thank you! YES! Dad's voice behind me barks.

They made me wear dad's hair-oil to look 'smart'.
A parting scored the grease like some slash scar.
Such aspirations hair might have for ART
were lopped, and licked by dollops from his jar.

And if the page I'm writing on has smears
they're not the sort to lose me marks for mess
being self-examination's grudging tears
soaked into the blotter, Nothingness,
on seeing the first still I'd ever seen
of Rudolph Valentino, father, O
now, *now* I know why you used *Brilliantine*
to slick back your black hair so long ago.

Background Material

My writing desk. Two photos, mam and dad.
A birthday, him. Their ruby wedding, her.
Neither one a couple and both bad.
I make out what's behind them from the blur.

Dad's in our favourite pub, now gone for good.
My father and his background are both gone,
but hers has my Welsh cottage and a wood
that still shows those same greens eight summers on,
though only the greenness of it 's stayed the same.

Though one of them 's in colour and one 's not,
the two are joined, apart from their shared frame,
by what, for photographers, would mar each shot:

in his, if you look close, the gleam, the light,
me in his blind right eye, but minute size –

in hers, as though just cast from where I write,
a shadow holding something to its eyes.

Self Justification

Me a poet! My daughter with maimed limb
became a more than tolerable sprinter.
And Uncle Joe. Impediment spurred him,
the worst stammerer I've known, to be a printer.

He handset type much faster than he spoke.
Those cruel consonants, *m*s, *p*s, and *b*s
on which his jaws and spirit almost broke
flicked into order with sadistic ease.

It seems right that Uncle Joe, 'b-buckshee
from the works', supplied those scribble pads
on which I stammered my first poetry
that made me seem a cissy to the lads.

Their aggro towards me, my need of them 's
what keeps my would-be mobile tongue still tied –

aggression, struggle, loss, blank printer's ems
by which all   eloquence   gets justified.

Bringing Up

It was a library copy otherwise
you'd've flung it in the fire in disgust.
Even cremation can't have dried the eyes
that wept for weeks about my 'sordid lust'.

The undertaker would have thought me odd
or I'd've put my book in your stiff hand.
You'd've been embarrassed though to meet your God
clutching those poems of mine that you'd like banned.

I thought you could hold my *Loiners*, and both burn!

And there together in the well wrought urn,
what's left of you, the poems of your child,
devoured by one flame, unreconciled,
like soots on washing, black on bone-ash white,

Maybe you see them in a better light!

But I still see you weeping, your hurt looks:

You weren't brought up to write such mucky books!

Lines to My Grandfathers

I

Ploughed parallel as print the stony earth.
The straight stone walls defy the steep grey slopes.
The place's rightness for my mother's birth
exceeds the pilgrim grandson's wildest hopes –

Wilkinson farmed Thrang Crag, Martindale.

Horner was the Haworth signalman.

Harrison kept a pub with home-brewed ale:

fell farmer, railwayman, and *publican*,

and he, while granma slaved to tend the vat
graced the rival bars 'to make comparisons',
Queen's Arms, the Duke of this, the Duke of that,
while his was known as just 'The Harrisons''.

He carried cane and *guineas*, no coin baser!
He dressed the gentleman beyond his place
and paid in gold for beer and whisky chaser
but took his knuckleduster, 'just in case'.

II

The one who lived with us was grampa Horner
who, I remember, when a sewer rat
got driven into our dark cellar corner
booted it to pulp and squashed it flat.

He cobbled all our boots. I've got his last.
We use it as a doorstop on warm days.
My present is propped open by their past
and looks out over straight and narrow ways:

the way one ploughed his land, one squashed a rat,
kept railtracks clear, or, dressed up to the nines,
with waxed moustache, gold chain, his cane, his hat,
drunk as a lord could foot it on straight lines.

Fell farmer, railwayman and publican,
I strive to keep my lines direct and straight,
and try to make connections where I can –

the knuckleduster's now my paperweight!

Remains

for Robert Woof and Fleur Adcock

Though thousands traipse round Wordsworth's Lakeland
     shrine
imbibing bardic background, they don't see
nailed behind a shutter one lost line
with intimations of mortality
and immortality, but so discrete
it's never trespassed on 'the poet's' aura,
nor been scanned, as it is, five strong verse feet.

W. Martin's work needs its restorer,
and so from 1891 I use
the paperhanger's one known extant line
as the culture that I need to start off mine
and honour his one visit by the Muse,
then hide our combined labours underground
so once again it might be truly said
in words from Grasmere written by the dead:

our heads will be happen cold when this is found.

W. Martin
paperhanger
4 July 1891

A Kumquat for John Keats

Today I found the right fruit for my prime,
not orange, not tangelo, and not lime,
nor moon-like globes of grapefruit that now hang
outside our bedroom, nor tart lemon's tang
(though last year full of bile and self-defeat
I wanted to believe no life was sweet)
nor the tangible sunshine of the tangerine,
and no incongruous citrus ever seen
at greengrocers' in Newcastle or Leeds
mis-spelt by the spuds and mud-caked swedes,
a fruit an older poet might substitute
for the grape John Keats thought fit to be Joy's fruit,
when, two years before he died, he tried to write
how Melancholy dwelled inside Delight,
and if he'd known the citrus that I mean
that's not orange, lemon, lime or tangerine,
I'm pretty sure that Keats, though he had heard
'of candied apple, quince and plum and gourd'
instead of 'grape against the palate fine'
would have, if he'd known it, plumped for mine,
this Eastern citrus scarcely cherry size
he'd bite just once and then apostrophise
and pen one stanza how the fruit had all
the qualities of fruit before the Fall,
but in the next few lines be forced to write
how Eve's apple tasted at the second bite,
and if John Keats had only lived to be,
because of extra years, in need like me,
at 42 he'd help me celebrate
that Micanopy kumquat that I ate
whole, straight off the tree, sweet pulp and sour skin –

or was it sweet outside, and sour within?
For however many kumquats that I eat
I'm not sure if it's flesh or rind that's sweet,
and being a man of doubt at life's mid-way
I'd offer Keats some kumquats and I'd say:
You'll find that one part's sweet and one part's tart:
say where the sweetness or the sourness start.

I find I can't, as if one couldn't say
exactly where the night became the day,
which makes for me the kumquat taken whole
best fruit, and metaphor, to fit the soul
of one in Florida at 42 with Keats
crunching kumquats, thinking, as he eats
the flesh, the juice, the pith, the pips, the peel,
that this is how a full life ought to feel,
its perishable relish prick the tongue,
when the man who savours life's no longer young,
the fruits that were his futures far behind.
Then it's the kumquat fruit expresses best
how days have darkness round them like a rind,
life has a skin of death that keeps its zest.

History, a life, the heart, the brain
flow to the taste buds and flow back again.
That decade or more past Keats's span
makes me an older not a wiser man,
who knows that it's too late for dying young,
but since youth leaves some sweetnesses unsung,
he's granted days and kumquats to express
Man's Being ripened by his Nothingness.
And it isn't just the gap of sixteen years,
a bigger crop of terrors, hopes and fears,
but a century of history on this earth

between John Keats's death and my own birth –
years like an open crater, gory, grim,
with bloody bubbles leering at the rim;
a thing no bigger than an urn explodes
and ravishes all silence, and all odes,
Flora asphyxiated by foul air
unknown to either Keats or Lemprière,
dehydrated Naiads, Dryad amputees
dragging themselves through slagscapes with no trees,
a shirt of Nessus fire that gnaws and eats
children half the age of dying Keats . . .

Now were you twenty five or six years old
when that fevered brow at last grew cold?
I've got no books to hand to check the dates.
My grudging but glad spirit celebrates
that all I've got to hand 's the kumquats, John,
the fruit I'd love to have your verdict on,
but dead men don't eat kumquats, or drink wine,
they shiver in the arms of Proserpine,
not warm in bed beside their Fanny Brawne,
nor watch her pick ripe grapefruit in the dawn
as I did, waking, when I saw her twist,
with one deft movement of a sunburnt wrist,
the moon, that feebly lit our last night's walk
past alligator swampland, off its stalk.
I thought of moon-juice juleps when I saw,
as if I'd never seen the moon before,
the planet glow among the fruit, and its pale light
make each citrus on the tree its satellite.

Each evening when I reach to draw the blind
stars seem the light zest squeezed through night's black
    rind;

the night's peeled fruit the sun, juiced of its rays,
first stains, then streaks, then floods the world with days,
days, when the very sunlight made me weep,
days, spent like the nights in deep, drugged sleep,
days in Newcastle by my daughter's bed,
wondering if she, or I, weren't better dead,
days in Leeds, grey days, my first dark suit,
my mother's wreaths stacked next to Christmas fruit,
and days, like this in Micanopy. Days!

As strong sun burns away the dawn's grey haze
I pick a kumquat and the branches spray
cold dew in my face to start the day.
The dawn's molasses make the citrus gleam
still in the orchards of the groves of dream.

The limes, like Galway after weeks of rain,
glow with a greenness that is close to pain,
the dew-cooled surfaces of fruit that spent
all last night flaming in the firmament.
The new day dawns. O days! My spirit greets
the kumquat with the spirit of John Keats.
O kumquat, comfort for not dying young,
both sweet and bitter, bless the poet's tongue!
I burst the whole fruit chilled by morning dew
against my palate. Fine, for 42!

I search for buzzards as the air grows clear
and see them ride fresh thermals overhead.
Their bleak cries were the first sound I could hear
when I stepped at the start of sunrise out of doors,
and a noise like last night's bedsprings on our bed
from Mr Fowler sharpening farmers' saws.

Cypress & Cedar

A smell comes off my pencil as I write
in the margins of a sacred Sanskrit text.
By just sufficient candlelight I skim
these scriptures sceptically from hymn to hymn.
The bits I read aloud to you I've Xed
for the little clues they offer to life's light.

I sit in mine, and you sit in your chair.
A sweetness hangs round yours; a foul smell mine.
Though the house still has no windows and no doors
and the tin roof's roughly propped with 4 × 4s
that any gale could jolt, our chairs are fine
and both scents battle for the same night air.

Near Chiefland just off US 129,
from the clapboard abattoir about a mile,
the local sawyer Bob displays his wares:
porch swings, picnic tables, lounging chairs,
rough sawn and nailed together 'cracker' style.
The hand I shake leaves powerful smells on mine.

Beside two piles of shavings, white and red,
one fragrant as a perfume, and one rank
and malodorous from its swampland ooze,
Bob displayed that week's work's chairs for me to choose.
I chose one that was sweet, and one that stank,
and thought about the sweet wood for a bed.

To quote the carpenter he 'stinks o' shite'
and his wife won't sleep with him on cypress days,
but after a day of cedar, so he said,

77

she comes back eagerly into his bed,
and, as long as he works cedar, there she stays.
Sometimes he scorns the red wood and works white!

Today I've laboured with my hands for hours
sawing fenceposts up for winter; one tough knot
jolted the chainsaw at my face and sprayed
a beetroot cedar dust off the bucked blade,
along with damp earth with its smell of rot,
hurtling beetles, termites in shocked showers.

To get one gatepost free I had to tug
for half an hour, but dragged up from its hole
it smelled, down even to the last four feet
rammed in the ground, still beautifully sweet
as if the grave had given life parole
and left the sour earth perfumed where I'd dug.

Bob gave me a cedar buckle for my belt,
and after the whole day cutting, stacking wood,
damp denim, genitals, 'genuine hide leather'
all these fragrances were bound together
by cedar, and together they smelled good.
It was wonderful the way my trousers smelled.

I can't help but suppose flesh-famished Phèdre
would have swept that prissy, epicene,
big-game hunting stepson Hippolyte,
led by his nose to cedar, off his feet,
and left no play at all for poor Racine,
if she'd soaped her breasts with *Bois de Cèdre*.

If in doubt ask Bob the sawyer's wife!
Pet lovers who can't stand the stink of cat

buy sacks of litter that's been 'cedarized'
and from ancient times the odour's been much prized.
Though not a Pharaoh I too favour that
for freighting my rank remains out of this life.

Why not two cedar chairs? Why go and buy
a reeking cypress chair as a reminder,
as if one's needed, of primeval ooze,
like swamps near Suwannee backroads, or bayous,
stagnation Mother Nature left behind her
hauling Mankind up from mononuclei?

Cypress still has roots in that old stew
paddling its origins in protozoa,
the stew where consciousness that writes and reads
grew its first squat tail from slimy seeds.
I'd've used it for the Ark if I'd been Noah,
though cedar, I know you'll say, would also do.

This place not in the *Blue Guide* or in *Fodor*
between the Suwannee River and the Styx
named by some homesick English classicist
who loved such puns, loathed swamps, and, lonely, pissed
his livelihood away with redneck hicks
and never once enjoyed the cedar's odour,

or put its smoke to snake-deterrent use
prescribed by Virgil in his *Georgics* III
with *chelydrus* here in the US South
construed as the diamondback or cottonmouth
which freed him, some said, from his misery.
Others said liquor, and others still a noose.

And, evenings, he, who'd been an avid reader
of the *Odyssey* and *Iliad* in Greek,
became an even avider verandah drinker
believing sourmash made a Stoic thinker
though stuck with no paddle up Phlegethon's creek,
and had no wife with clothes chest of sweet cedar.

But you bought one at Bob's place and you keep
your cotton frocks in it, your underwear,
and such a fragrance comes from your doffed bras
as come from uncorked phials in hot bazaars,
and when you take your clothes off and lie bare
your body breathes out cedar while you sleep.

That lonely English exile named the river,
though it could have been someone like me, for whom,
though most evenings on the porch I read and write,
there's often such uneasiness in night
it creates despair in me, or drinker's gloom
that could send later twinges through the liver.

Tonight so far 's been peaceful with no lightning.
The pecan trees and hophornbeams are still.
The storm's held off, the candleflame's quite straight,
the fire and wick united in one fate.
Though this quietness that can, one moment, fill
the heart with peace, can, the next, be frightening –

A hog gets gelded with a gruesome squeal
that skids across the quietness of night
to where we're sitting on our dodgy porch.
I reach for Seth Tooke's shotgun and the torch
then realise its 'farmwork' so alright
but my flesh also flinches from the steel.

Peace like a lily pad on swamps of pain –
floating's its only way of being linked.
This consciousness of ours that reads and writes
drifts on a darkness deeper than the night's.
Above that blackness, buoyed on the extinct,
peace, pure-white, floats flowering in the brain,

and fades, as finally the nenuphar
we found on a pewter swamp where two roads ended
was also bound to fade. The head and heart
are neither of them too much good apart
and peace comes in the moments that they're blended
as cypress and cedar at this moment are.

My love, as prone as I am to despair,
I think the world of night's best born in pairs,
one half we'll call the female, one the male,
though neither essence need, in love, prevail.
We sit here in distinctly scented chairs
you, love, in the cedar, me the cypress chair.

Though tomorrow night I might well sit in yours
and you in mine, the blended scent's the same
since I pushed my chair close to your chair
and we read by the one calm candle that we share
in this wilderness that might take years to tame,
this house still with no windows and no doors.

Let the candle cliché come out of the chill –
'the flickering candle on a vast dark plain'
of one lone voice against the state machine,
or Mimi's on cold stairs aren't what I mean
but moments like this now when heart and brain
seem one sole flame that's bright and straight and still.

If it's in Levy County that I die
(though fearing I'd feel homesick as I died
I'd sooner croak in Yorkshire if I could)
I'll have my coffin made of cedar wood
to balance the smell like cypress from inside
and hope the smoke of both blends in the sky,

as both scents from our porch chairs do tonight.
'Tvashti', says this Indian Rig Veda,
'hewed the world out of one tree,' but doesn't tell,
since for durability both do as well,
if the world he made was cypress wood; or cedar
the smell coming off my pencil as I write.

Anne Stevenson

The Marriage

They will fit, she thinks,
but only if her backbone
cuts exactly into his rib cage,
and only if his knees
dock exactly under her knees
and all four
agree on a common angle.

All would be well
if only
they could face each other.

Even as it is
there are compensations
for having to meet
nose to neck
chest to scapula
groin to rump
when they sleep.

They look, at least,
as if they were going
in the same direction.

With My Sons at Boarhills

Gulls think it is for them
that the wormy sand rises,
brooding on its few rights,
losing its war with water.

The mussel flats ooze out,
and now the barnacled, embossed
stacked rocks are pedestals for strangers,
for my own strange sons,
scraping in the pool,
imperilling their pure reflections.

Their bodies are less beautiful than
blue heaven's pleiades of herring gulls,
or gannets, or that sloop's sail
sawtoothing the sea as if its
scenery were out of date, as if its
photographs had all been taken:
two boys left naked in a sloughed off summer,
skins and articulate backbones,
fossils for scrapbook or cluttered mantelpiece.

If you look now, quickly and askance,
you can see how the camera's eye
perfected what was motion and chance before
it clicked on this day, and childhood snapshot,
scarcely seen beside
hunched rugby stripes and ugly uniforms –
shy, familiar grins in a waste of faces.

My knee joints ache and crack

as I kneel to my room's fire, feeding it.
Steam wreathes from my teacup, clouding
the graduate, the lieutenant, the weddings,
the significant man of letters, the politician
smiling from his short victory . . .

Faces I washed and scolded, only
watched as my each child laboured from his own womb,
bringing forth, without me, men who must
call me mother, love or reassess me
as their barest needs dictate, return
dreaming, rarely to this saltpool in memory,
naked on a morning full of see-through jellyfish,
with the tide out and the gulls out
grazing on healed beaches,
while sea-thrift blazes by the dry path,
and the sail stops cutting the water to pieces
and heads for some named port inland.

Their voices return like footprints over the sandflats,
permanent, impermanent, salt and sensuous
as the sea is, in its frame, its myth.

The Three

In this picture I preside. I usher in
river and bathers, the green garden.
This tall white birch is my lively cocoon.
Out of it I spin chervils – marriages, babies.
All my blown hair is seed, is a tide in bloom,
furious as history, indifferent as it is.

In this picture I persuade. I lead men in,
conduct them through the garden.
Composed, smooth-headed in my spidery greys,
I drop their lines precisely, deploy them
precisely. These are the criers out in my displays.
Their outrage burns in words as I destroy them.

In this last picture I work alone.
I kill roots to plant stone.
I bring to hard soil no fruit, no hurt.
No cry issues from my burnt hillside.
Green burden and echo wait under my foot
for the igneous reaches, the granite tide.

If I Could Paint Essences

Another day in March. Late
rawness and wetness. I hear my mind say,
if only I could paint essences ...

such as the mudness of mud
on this rainsoaked dyke where coltsfoot
displays its yellow misleading daisy;

such as the westness of west here
in England's last thatched, rivered
county. Red ploughland. Green pasture.

Black cattle. Quick water. Overpainted
by lightshafts from layered gold
and purple cumulus. A cloudness of clouds

which are not like anything but clouds.

But just as I arrive at true sightness of seeing,
unexpectedly I want to play on those bell-toned
cellos of delicate not-quite-flowering larches

that offer on the opposite hill their unfurled
amber instruments – floating, insubstantial, a rising
horizon of music embodied in light.

And in such imaginings I lose sight of sight.
Just as I will lose the tune of what
hurls in my head, as I turn back, turn

ANNE STEVENSON

home to you, conversation, the inescapable ache
of trying to catch, say, the catness of cat
as he crouches, stalking his shadow,

on the other side of the window.

The Garden

She feels it like a shoulder of hair,
the garden, shrugging off the steamed, squeezed
eye of her kitchen window. Self-engendered chaos,
milky convolvulus, huge comet daisies. Tear
open the stocking of the leek pod and it frees
mathematically its globe, its light radiants.

But still she feels it hateful, August in its sweat,
the children filthy and barefoot . . . angry woman
in a stained striped apron, sipping juice off a knife,
thick syrups of pounded rose hip and pulped fruit.
In bright air, between briar roses and a viney drain,
Arenea diadema sips the silk-spindled fly.

Her pet cat's a killer, a fur muff
curled fatly now in a catnest of hot
grass and goutweed. Of this morning's robin
too much was left – feathers, fluff
feet, beak, the gorgeous throat caught
in the gored, delicate, perfectly balanced skeleton.

Poem to My Daughter

'I think I'm going to have it,'
I said, joking between pains.
The midwife rolled competent
sleeves over corpulent milky arms.
'Dear, you never have it,
we deliver it.'
A judgement years proved true.
Certainly I've never had you

as you still have me, Caroline.
Why does a mother need a daughter?
Heart's needle – hostage to fortune –
freedom's end. Yet nothing's more perfect
than that bleating, razor-shaped cry
that delivers a mother to her baby.
The bloodcord snaps that held
their sphere together. The child,
tiny and alone, creates the mother.

A woman's life is her own
until it is taken away
by a first particular cry.
Then she is not alone
but a part of the premises
of everything there is.
A branch, a tide . . . a war.
When we belong to the world
we become what we are.

Buzzard and Alder

Buzzard that folds itself into and becomes nude
alder; alder that insensibly becomes bird –
one life inside the dazzling tree. Together
they do change everything, and forever.

You think, because no news is said here,
not. But rain's rained weather to a rare
blue, so you can see the thinness of it,
I mean the layer they live in, flying in it,

breaking through it minute by glass minute.
Buzzard, hunched in disuse before it
shatters winter, wheeling after food.
Alder, silently glazing us, the dead.

Taking Down the Christmas Tree

Twelve days, twelve nights, and another Christmas is lost.
The dead spruce is dismantled, its costume of
shining but each year's more shabbily resurrected angels
        is undone at last,
is returned globe by globe, horse by gaudy little
brocade horse, star, and incandescent sequined dove
        to the recurring past.

And now the room is being groomed and put together
by this same brisk hand and snorting machine that
helplessly prepared its dazzle. The children, who came
        home like squally weather,
human in the storm of everything they expected to be
marvellous, would not call this 'Christmas'. But it's the
        same thing as the other,

this sweeping up, implicit in the dangerous promise
of celebration we, almost without thinking, risk
at the winter solstice, bringing the cold forest
        into the warm house.
This harvest of spiny unlooked for needles is almost
seed; and the victim, decked out for worship, is at last
        lost, sacrificed,

so the rite of birth can be death's from the beginning.
What can I say to this sixteen-year-old who packs up
his music patiently and crams for Oxford? Or to Maya at
        ten who minds not winning
at Scrabble but is brave about it? 'The putting up
and taking down of a tree are in time one action,
        as the spring

92

is one action with autumn, and winter with summer?'
I breathe thanks, instead, to the vacuum cleaner which
prevents too much metaphysics and mother-tears. But the
    tree will not all disappear.
In April I'll trace it again, I know, beating these carpets.
Or, lazing in August and stung by what should be a bee,
    I'll pull spruce from my hair.

In the Tunnel of Summers

Moving from day into day
I don't know how,
eating these plums now
this morning for breakfast
tasting of childhood's
mouth-pucker tartness,
watching the broad light
seed in the fences,
honey of barley,
gold ocean, grasses,
as the tunnel of summers,
of nothing but summers,
opens again
in my travelling senses.

I am eight and eighteen and eighty
all the Augusts of my day.

Why should I be, I be
more than another?
brown foot in sandal,
burnt palm on flaked clay,
flesh under waterfall
baubled in strong spray,
blood on the stubble
of fly-sweet hay –
why not my mother's, my
grandmother's ankle
hurting as harvest hurts
thistle and animal?
a needle of burning,
why this way or that way?

They are already building the long straw cemetery
where my granddaughter's daughter has been born and
buried.

Making Poetry

'You have to inhabit poetry
if you want to make it.'

And what's 'to inhabit'?

To be in the habit of, to wear
words, sitting in the plainest light,
in the silk of morning, in the shoe of night;
a feeling, bare and frondish in surprising air;
familiar ... rare.

And what's 'to make'?

To be and to become words' passing
weather; to serve a girl on terrible
terms, embark on voyages over voices,
evade the ego-hill, the misery-well,
the siren hiss of *publish, success, publish,
success, success, success.*

And why inhabit, make, inherit poetry?

Oh, it's the shared comedy of the worst
blessed; the sound leading the hand;
a wordlife running from mind to mind
through the washed rooms of the simple senses;
one of those haunted, undefendable, unpoetic
crosses we have to find.

Spring Song of the Poet-Housewife

The sun is warm,
and the house in the sun
is filthy ...

grime like a permanent fog
    on the soot-framed windowpanes,
dust, imprinted with cat's feet,
    on the lid of the hi-fi,
dishes on the dresser
    in a deepening plush of disuse,
books on the blackened shelves,
    bearing in the cusps of their pages
    a stripe of mourning ...

The sun is warm,
the dust motes and dust mice
are dancing,

the ivies are pushing green tongues
    from their charcoal tentacles,
the fire is reduced to a
    smoky lamp in a cave.
Soon it will be spring, sweet spring,
    and I will take pleasure in spending
many hours and days out of doors,
    away from the chores and bores
    of these filthy things.

A Prayer to Live with Real People

Let me not live, ever, without fat people,
the marshmallow flesh set thick on the muscular bone,
the silk white perms of sweet sixteen-stone ladies,
luscious as pom-poms or full blown perfumed magnolias,
with breasts like cottage loaves dropped into lace-knit
    sweaters,
all cream-bun arms and bottoms in sticky leathers.
O Russian dolls, O range of hills
rosy behind the glo-green park of the pool table,
thorns are not neater or sharper than your delicate shoes.

Let me not live, ever, without pub people,
the tattooed forearm steering the cue like a pencil,
the twelve-pint belly who adds up the scores in his head,
the wiry owner of whippets, the keeper of ferrets,
thin wives who suffer, who are silent, who talk with their
    eyes,
the girl who's discovered that sex is for she who tries.
O zebra blouse, O vampish back

Let me live always and forever among neighbours like these
who order their year by the dates of the leek competitions,
who care sacrificially for Jack Russell terriers and pigeons,
who read very carefully captions in *The Advertiser* and *Echo*
which record their successes and successes of teams they
    support,
whose daughters grow up and marry friends' boys from
    Crook.
O wedding gifts, O porcelain flowers
twined on their vases under the lacelip curtains,
save me from Habitat and snobbery and too damn much
    literary ambition!

The Other House

In the house of childhood
I looked up to my mother's face;
the sturdy roofbeam of her smile
buckled the rooms in place.
A shape of the unchangeable
    taught me the word 'gone'.

In the house of growing up
I lined my prison wall
with lives I worshipped as I read.
If I chose one, I chose all,
such paper clothes I coveted
    and ached to try on.

The house of youth has a grand door,
a ruin the other side
where death watch & company
compete with groom and bride.
Nothing was what seemed to be
    in that charged dawn.

They advertised the house of love,
I bought the house of pain,
with shabby little wrongs and rights
where beams should have been.
How could those twisted splintered nights
    stand up alone?

My angry house was a word house,
a city of the brain,

where buried heads and salt gods
struggled to breathe again.
Into those echoing, sealed arcades
    I hurled a song.

It glowed with an electric pulse,
firing the sacred halls.
Bright reproductions of itself
travelled the glassy walls.
'Ignis fatuus', cried my voice.
    And I moved on.

I drove my mind to a strange house
infinitely huge and small,
a cone, to which a dew-drop earth
leeches, invisible.
Infinite steps of death and birth
    lead up and down.

Beneath me, infinitely deep,
solidity dissolves;
above me, infinitely wide,
galactic winter sprawls.
That house of the utterly outside
    became my home.

In it, the house of childhood
safeguards my mother's face.
A lifted eyebrow's 'Yes, and so?'
latches the rooms in place.
I tell my children all I know
    of the word 'gone'.

Elegy

Whenever my father was left with nothing to do—
    waiting for someone to 'get ready',
or facing the gap between graduate seminars
    and dull after-suppers in his study
grading papers or writing a review—
    he played the piano.

I think of him packing his lifespan
    carefully, like a good leather briefcase,
each irritating chore wrapped in floating passages
    for the left hand and right hand
by Chopin or difficult Schumann;
    nothing inside it ever rattled loose.

Not rationalism, though you could cut your tongue
    on the blade of his reasonable logic.
Only at the piano did he become
    the bowed, reverent, wholly absorbed Romantic.
The theme of his heroic, unfinished piano sonata
    could have been Brahms.

Boredom, or what he disapproved of as
    'sitting around with your mouth open'
oddly pursued him. He had small stamina.
    Whenever he succumbed to bouts of winter bronchitis
the house sank a little into its snowed-up garden,
    missing its musical swim-bladder.

None of this suggests how natural he was.
    For years I thought fathers played the piano
just as dogs barked and babies grew.

We children ran in and out of the house,
taking for granted that the 'Trout' or E flat Major
    Impromptu would be rippling around us.

For him, I think, playing was solo flying, a bliss
    of removal, of being alone.
Not happily always; never an escape,
    for he was affectionate, and the household hum
he pretended to find trivial or ridiculous
    daily sustained him.

When he talked about music, it was never
    of the *lachrimae rerum*
that trembled from his drawn-out phrasing
    as raindrops phrase themselves along a wire;
no, he defended movable doh or explained the amazing
    physics of the octave.

We'd come in from school and find him
    crossed-legged on the jungle of the floor,
guts from one of his Steinways strewn about him.
    He always got the pieces back in place.
I remember the yellow covers of Schirmer's Editions
    and the bound Peters Editions in the bookcase.

When he defected to the cello in later years
    Grandmother, *in excrucio*, mildly exclaimed,
'Wasn't it lovely when Steve liked to play the piano.'
    Now I'm the grandmother listening to Steve at the piano.
Lightly, in strains from the Brahms-Haydn variations,
    his audible image returns to my humming ears.

Welsh Pastoral

For my grandson, 10 March, 1988

After it had rained all winter
April brought a chill East wind.
Somehow the sun got used to it
and stayed cheerful. In kind
(for Wales) well-mannered weather,
daffodils stretched and unfurled.
New lambs slipped out of their mothers
into a washed world.
Soon clumps of them could be seen
like quartz or distant cataracts
on hills not yet hospitable
but intensely green.

Driving from Llanfihangel on the A496
we stopped by a minor pasture where a shivery
minute-old calf had just introduced himself
to the terrible twentieth century.
He lay on the rough mud amazed, while
his mother licked off the salt envelope.
Behind her a rose red umbilicus
hanging down like a second tail
held and repelled us.

Of course we wanted to see
if the herd, closing in, could help.
But cows take their time over
rites of assent or hostility,
and we were, of course, in a hurry.

So we never saw the calf get up
from its grab-bag of legs to suck,
or knew how its mother worked free
of that long, necessary,
embarrassingly tough red rope.

Stone Fig

The young fig tree feels with its hands
along the white sunny wall
and at the end of August
produces seven fruits,
seven royal fists that will be
runny with seed, ripe
with a musky honey that rarefies sweetness.

For the sick woman in the bedroom
behind the all-day-drawn curtains
I set the fruit in the sun
by the kitchen window.
Seven brimming wineskins
and a flint from the garden
she must have collected with a smile,
for it looks exactly like a fig.

A stone fig,
a hard, smooth, comfort-in-the-hand
Platonic Idea of Fig.

I watch the others daily for readiness;
this one, and now that one.

As if they were the last of her feelings
the old lady gobbles the ripe figs.

Quickly, quickly, such greediness.
She eats them like anaesthetic.
Here's pith in her pale fingernails,
purple on the stubble of her chin.

Her legs are dry twigs. She can't
trust them to take her to the toilet,
then back again. Her skin is mottled
with overripeness I look away from.

She wants, she smiles, to sleep
and sleep and sleep. And then
to sleep again.

What I Miss

is some hexagonal white seal
like a honeycell.
Silence I miss;
the hand on the fiddle
muting the vaulted arrogance
it raises;
the crowded hush
of the conductor's lifted wand,
then the chorale
walking with little empty breaths
through air it praises.

My air is noises
amplified by an ugly pink
barnacle in my ear.
All the music I hear
is a tide dragging pebbles
to and away in my brain.
Sphered, the harmonies fall,
mutate, abort. Emptiness
is like rain
in my insomniac city,
ceaseless and merciless.

For Elon Salmon

From the Motorway

Everywhere up and down the island
Britain is mending her desert;
marvellous we exclaim as we fly on it,
tying the country in a parcel,
London to Edinburgh, Birmingham to Cardiff,
No time to examine the contents,

thank you, but consider the bliss of
sitting absolutely numbed to your
nulled mind, music when you want it,
while identical miles thunder under you,
the same spot coming and going
seventy, eighty times a minute,

till you're there, wherever there
is, ready to be someone in
Liverpool, Leeds, Manchester,
they're all the same to the road,
which loves itself, which nonetheless
here and there hands you trailing

necklaces of fumes in which to be
one squeezed breather among
rich and ragged, sprinter and staggerer,
a status parade for Major Roadworks
toiling in his red-trimmed triangle,
then a regiment of wounded orange witches

defending a shamelessly naked
(rarely a stitch of work on her)
captive free lane,
while the inchlings inch on
without bite or sup, at most
a hard shoulder to creep on,

while there, on all sides,
lie your unwrapped destinations,
lanes trickling off into childhood
or anonymity, apple-scented villages
asleep in their promise of being
nowhere anyone would like to get to.

Journal Entry: Impromptu in C Minor

Edinburgh, October, 1988

After weeks of October drench,
a warm orange day,
a conflagration of all the trees and streets in Edinburgh.

Let me have no thoughts
in this weather of pure sensation.

Getting into the car is a coatless sensation.
Driving through the traffic
is the feeling of falling leaves.

The Firth, like the sky, is blue, blue,
with sandy brown puffs of surf on the oily beaches.
The sea swell rises and spills,
rises and spills, tumbling its load of crockery
without breakage.

Is a metaphor a thought?
Then let these shells be shells,
those sharp white sails be sails.

Today the pink enormous railway bridge,
is neither a three-humped camel nor a dinosaur
but a grand feat of Scottish engineering;
now and then it rumbles peacefully
as a tiny train, rather embarrassed, scuttles across it.

Sitting with pure sensation on the breakwater,
I unhook the wires of my mind.
I undo the intellectual spider's web.
Uncomplicated me.

But I correct myself.
Soon I'm standing in my grid of guilts
hastily reaching for my thoughts.

For there are people out there.
Not abstractions, not ideas, but people.
In the black, beyond the blue of my perception,
in the huge vault where the wires won't reach,
the dead are lively.
The moment I take off my thought-clothes
I expose every nerve to their waves.

What is this sad marching melody?
A spy, a column on reconnaissance,
the theme from Schubert's Impromptu in C minor.

It is 1943.
In a frame house that has forgotten him,
a dead man is playing the piano.
I am ten years old. For the first time
I watch a grown woman weep.
Her husband, the white-haired Jewish philosopher,
makes shy mistakes in English.
He puts an arm around his wife
and bows his head.

The theme returns years later
to a farmhouse in Vermont.

This time I myself am at the piano,
a puzzled girl I instantly recognise
although she died through more years than Schubert lived
to make room for the woman I am now.

I smile at her ambition.
She doesn't yet know she will be deaf.

She doesn't yet know how deaf she's been.

What is the matter?

This is the matter: deafness and deadness.
The shoe-heaps, hills of fillings, children's bones.
Headlines blacking out the breakfast chatter;
        (We go on eating).
Static and foreign voices on the radio;
        (We are late for school).

Then silence folding us in,
folding them under.

But here is the melody.

And here, 'our daemonic century'
in which a dead man's dead march
plays itself over and over
on a fine fall day in South Queensferry
in the head of a fortunate (though deaf) American
    grandmother

She sits in the momentary sun looking at the sea.

Once there lived in Austria a schoolmaster's son,
shy, myopic, a little stout, but lucky,
for his talent was exactly suited to his time.
Careless of his health in an age of medical ignorance,
he died at thirty-one, probably of syphilis.
A few moments of his life, five notes of it,
fuse with a few impromptu responses,
a few contemporary cells.

They provide the present and future
of an every-minute dying planet
with a helix, a hinge of survival.

Eros

I call for love
But, help me, who arrives?
This thug with broken nose
And squinty eyes.
'Eros, my bully boy,
Can this be you,
With boxer lips
And patchy wings askew?'

'Madam', cries Eros,
'Know the brute you see
Is what long over use
Has made of me.
My face that so offends you
Is the sum
Of blows your lust delivered
One by one.

We slaves who are immortal
Gloss your fate,
And are the archetypes
That you create.
Better my battered visage,
Bruised but hot,
Than love dissolved in loss
Or left to rot.'

Derek Walcott

Ruins of a Great House

though our longest sun sets at right declensions and makes but
winter arches, it cannot be long before we lie down in darkness,
and have our light in ashes . . .

BROWNE: Urn Burial

Stones only, the *disjecta membra* of this Great House,
Whose moth-like girls are mixed with candledust,
Remain to file the lizard's dragonish claws;
The mouths of those gate cherubs streaked with stain.
Axle and coachwheel silted under the muck
Of cattle droppings.

              Three crows flap for the trees,
And settle, creaking the eucalyptus boughs.
A smell of dead limes quickens in the nose
The leprosy of Empire.

           'Farewell, green fields'
           'Farewell, ye happy groves!'

Marble as Greece, like Faulkner's south in stone,
Deciduous beauty prospered and is gone;
But where the lawn breaks in a rash of trees
A spade below dead leaves will ring the bone
Of some dead animal or human thing
Fallen from evil days, from evil times.

It seems that the original crops were limes
Grown in the silt that clogs the river's skirt;
The imperious rakes are gone, their bright girls gone,
The river flows, obliterating hurt.

I climbed a wall with the grill ironwork
Of exiled craftsmen, protecting that great house
From guilt, perhaps, but not from the worm's rent,
Nor from the padded cavalry of the mouse.
And when a wind shook in the limes I heard
What Kipling heard; the death of a great empire, the abuse
Of ignorance by Bible and by sword.

A green lawn, broken by low walls of stone
Dipped to the rivulet, and pacing, I thought next
Of men like Hawkins, Walter Raleigh, Drake,
Ancestral murderers and poets, more perplexed
In memory now by every ulcerous crime.
The world's green age then was a rotting lime
Whose stench became the charnel galleon's text.
The rot remains with us, the men are gone.
But, as dead ash is lifted in a wind,
That fans the blackening ember of the mind,
My eyes burned from the ashen prose of Donne.

Ablaze with rage, I thought
Some slave is rotting in this manorial lake,
And still the coal of my compassion fought:
That Albion too, was once
A colony like ours, 'Part of the continent, piece of the main'
Nook-shotten, rook o'er blown, deranged
By foaming channels, and the vain expense
Of bitter faction.

        All in compassion ends
So differently from what the heart arranged:
'as well as if a manor of thy friend's . . .'

Missing the Sea

Something removed roars in the ears of this house,
Hangs its drapes windless, stuns mirrors
Till reflections lack substance.

Some sound like the gnashing of windmills ground
To a dead halt;
A deafening absence, a blow.

It hoops this valley, weighs this mountain,
Estranges gesture, pushes this pencil
Through a thick nothing now,

Freights cupboards with silence, folds sour laundry
Like the clothes of the dead left exactly
As the dead behaved by the beloved,

Incredulous, expecting occupancy.

Laventille

(*for V. S. Naipaul*)

To find the Western Path
Through the Gates of Wrath
                    Blake

It huddled there
steel tinkling its blue painted metal air,
tempered in violence, like Rio's favelas,

with snaking, perilous streets whose edges fell as
its episcopal turkey-buzzards fall
from its miraculous hilltop

shrine,
down the impossible drop
to Belmont, Woodbrook, Maraval, St Clair

that shine
like peddlers' tin trinkets in the sun.
From a harsh

shower, its gutters growled and gargled wash
past the Youth Centre, past the water catchment,
a rigid children's carousel of cement;

we climbed where lank electric
lines and tension cables linked its raw brick
hovels like a complex feud,

where the inheritors of the middle passage stewed
five to a room, still clamped below their hatch,
breeding like felonies,

whose lives revolve round prison, graveyard, church.
Below bent breadfruit trees
in the flat, coloured city, class

lay escalated into structures still,
merchant, middleman, magistrate, knight. To go downhill
from here was to ascend.

The middle passage never guessed its end.
This is the height of poverty
for the desperate and black;

climbing, we could look back
with widening memory
on the hot, corrugated iron sea
whose horrors we all

shared. The salt blood knew it well,
you, me, Samuel's daughter, Samuel,
and those ancestors clamped below its grate.

And climbing steeply past the wild
gutters, it shrilled
in the blood, for those who suffered, who were killed,

and who survive.
What other gift was there to give
as the godparents of his unnamed child?

Yet outside the brown annexe of the church, the
stifling odour of bay rum and talc, the particular,
neat sweetness of the crowd distressed

that sense. The black, fawning verger
his bow tie akimbo, grinning, the clown-gloved
fashionable wear of those I deeply loved

once, made me look on with hopelessness and rage
at their new, apish habits, their excess
and fear, the possessed, the self-possessed;

their perfume shrivelled to a childhood fear
of Sabbath graveyards, christenings, marriages,
that muggy, steaming, self-assuring air

of tropical Sabbath afternoons. And in
the church, eyes prickling with rage,
the children rescued from original sin

by their God-father since the middle passage,
the supercilious brown curate, who intones,

healing the guilt in these rachitic bones,
twisting my love within me like a knife,
'across the troubled waters of this life . . .'

Which of us cares to walk
even if God wished
those retching waters where our souls were fished

for this new world? Afterwards, we talk
in whispers, close to death
among these stones planted on alien earth.

119

Afterwards,
the ceremony, the careful photograph
moved out of range before the patient tombs,

we dare a laugh,
ritual, desperate words,
born like these children from habitual wombs,

from lives fixed in the unalterable groove
of grinding poverty. I stand out on a balcony
and watch the sun pave its flat, golden path

across the roofs, the aerials, cranes, the tops
of fruit trees crawling downward to the city.
Something inside is laid wide like a wound,

some open passage that has cleft the brain,
some deep, amnesiac blow. We left
somewhere a life we never found,

customs and gods that are not born again,
some crib, some grill of light
clanged shut on us in bondage, and withheld

us from that world below us and beyond,
and in its swaddling cerements we're still bound.

Mass Man

Through a great lion's head clouded by mange
a black clerk growls.
Next, a gold-wired peacock withholds a man,
a fan, flaunting its oval, jewelled eyes,
What metaphors!
What coruscating, mincing fantasies!

Hector Mannix, water-works clerk San Juan, has entered
   a lion,
Boysie, two golden mangoes bobbing for breastplates,
   barges
like Cleopatra down her river, making style.
'Join us' they shout, 'O God, child, you can't dance?'
but somewhere in that whirlwind's radiance
a child, rigged like a bat, collapses, sobbing.

But I am dancing, look, from an old gibbet
my bull-whipped body swings, a metronome!
Like a fruit-bat dropped in the silk cotton's shade
my mania, my mania is a terrible calm.

Upon your penitential morning,
some skull must rub its memory with ashes,
some mind must squat down howling in your dust,
some hand must crawl and recollect your rubbish,
someone must write your poems.

Homecoming: Anse La Raye

(*for Garth St Omer*)

Whatever else we learned
at school, like solemn Afro-Greeks eager for grades,
of Helen and the shades
of borrowed ancestors,
there are no rites
for those who have returned,
only, when her looms fade,
drilled in our skulls, the doom-
surge-haunted nights,
only this well-known passage
under the coconuts' salt-rusted
swords, these rotted
leathery sea-grape leaves,
the seacrabs' brittle helmets, and
this barbecue of branches, like the ribs
of sacrificial oxen on scorched sand;
only this fish-gut reeking beach
whose spindly, sugar-headed children race
whose starved, pot-bellied children race
pelting up from the shallows
because your clothes,
your posture
seem a tourist's.
They swarm like flies
round your heart's sore.

Suffer them to come,
entering your needle's eye,
knowing whether they live or die,

what others make of life will pass them by
like that far silvery freighter
threading the horizon like a toy;
for once, like them,
you wanted no career
but this sheer light, this clear,
infinite, boring, paradisal sea,
but hoped it would mean something to declare
today, I am your poet, yours,
all this you knew,
but never guessed you'd come.
to know there are homecomings without home.

You give them nothing.
Their curses melt in air.
The black cliffs scowl,
the ocean sucks its teeth,
like that dugout canoe
a drifting petal fallen in a cup,
with nothing but its image,
you sway, reflecting nothing.
The freighter's silvery ghost
is gone, the children gone.
Dazed by the sun
you trudge back to the village
past the white, salty esplanade
under whose palms, dead
fishermen move their draughts in shade,
crossing, eating their islands,
and one, with a politician's
ignorant, sweet smile, nods,
as if all fate
swayed in his lifted hand.

Guyana

I

The surveyor straightens from his theodolite.
'Spirit-level,' he scrawls, and instantly
the ciphers staggering down their columns
are soldier ants, their panic radiating in the shadow
of a new god arriving over Aztec anthills.

The sun has sucked his brain pith-dry.
His vision whirls with dervishes, he is dust.
Like an archaic photographer, hooded in shade,
he crouches, screwing a continent to his eye.

The vault that balances on a grass blade,
the nerve-cracked ground too close for the word
    'measureless',
for the lost concept, 'man',
revolve too slowly for the fob-watch of his world,
for the tidal markings of the five-year plan.

Ant-sized to God, god to an ant's eyes,
shouldering science he begins to tread
himself, a world that must be measured in three days.

The frothing shallows of the river,
the forest so distant that it tires of blue,
the merciless idiocy of green, green . . .

a shape dilates towards him through the haze.

Another Life

Chapter 2

II

          Maman,
only on Sundays was the Singer silent,
then
tobacco smelt stronger, was more masculine.
Sundays
the parlour smelt of uncles,
the lamp poles rang,
the drizzle shivered its maracas,
like mandolins the tightening wires of rain,
then
from striped picnic buses, *jour marron*,
gold bangles tinkled like good-morning in Guinea
and a whore's laughter opened like sliced fruit.

Maman,
you sat folded in silence,
as if your husband might walk up the street,
while in the forests the cicadas pedalled their machines,
and silence, a black maid in white,
barefooted, polished and repolished
the glass across his fading watercolours,
the dumb Victrola cabinet,
the panels and the gleam of blue-winged teal
beating the mirror's lake.
In silence,
the revered, silent objects ring like glass,

at my eyes' touch, everything tightened, tuned,
Sunday,
the dead Victrola;

Sunday, a child
breathing with lungs of bread;
Sunday, the sacred silence of machines.

Maman,
your son's ghost circles your lost house, looking in
incomprehensibly at its dumb tenants
like fishes busily inaudible behind glass,
while the carpenter's Gothic joke, A, W, A, W,
Warwick and Alix involved in its eaves
breaks with betrayal.
You stitched us clothes from the nearest elements,
made shirts of rain and freshly ironed clouds,
then, singing your iron hymn, you riveted
your feet on Monday to the old machine.

Then Monday plunged her arms up to the elbows
in a foam tub, under a blue-soap sky,
the wet fleets sailed the yard, and every bubble,
with its bent, mullioned window, opened
its mote of envy in the child's green eye
of that sovereign-headed, pink-cheeked bastard Bubbles
in the frontispiece of *Pears Cyclopedia*.
Rising in crystal spheres, world after world.

They melt from you, your sons.
Your arms grow full of rain.

Chapter 15

I

Still dreamt of, still missed,
especially on raw, rainy mornings, your face shifts
into anonymous schoolgirl faces, a punishment,
since sometimes you condescend to smile,
since at the corners of the smile there is forgiveness.

Besieged by sisters, you were a prize
of which they were too proud, circled
by the thorn thicket of their accusation,
what grave deep wrong, what wound have you brought,
    Anna?

The rain season comes with its load.
The half-year has travelled far. Its back hurts.
It drizzles wearily.

It is twenty years since,
after another war, the shell cases are where?
But in our brassy season, our imitation autumn,
your hair puts out its fire,
your gaze haunts innumerable photographs,

now clear, now indistinct,
all that pursuing generality,
that vengeful conspiracy with nature,

all that sly informing of objects,
and behind every line, your laugh
frozen into a lifeless photograph.

In that hair I could walk through the wheatfields of
    Russia,
your arms were downed and ripening pears,
for you became, in fact, another country,

you are Anna of the wheatfield and the weir,
you are Anna of the solid winter rain,
Anna of the smoky platform and the cold train,
in that war of absence, Anna of the steaming stations,

gone from the marsh edge,
from the drizzled shallows
puckering with gooseflesh,
Anna of the first green poems that startlingly hardened,

of the mellowing breasts now,
Anna of the lurching, long flamingoes
of the harsh salt lingering in the thimble
of the bather's smile,

Anna of the darkened house, among the reeking shell
    cases,
lifting my hand and swearing us to her breast,
unbearably clear-eyed.

You are all Annas, enduring all goodbyes,
within the cynical station of your body,
Christie, Karenina, big-boned and passive,

that I found life within some novel's leaves
more real than you, already chosen
as his doomed heroine. You knew, you knew.

The Harvest

If they ask what my favourite flower was,
there's one thing that you'll have to understand:
I learnt to love it by the usual ways
of those who swore to serve truth with one hand,
and one behind their back for cash or praise,
that I surrendered dreaming how I'd stand
in the rewarding autumn of my life,
just ankle-deep in money, thick as leaves,
to bring my poetry, poor, faithful wife
past her accustomed style, well, all the same,
though there's no autumn, nature played the game
with me each fiscal year, when the gold pouis
would guiltily start scattering largesse
like Christian bankers or wind-shook-down thieves.
What I soon learnt was they had changed the script,
left out the golden fall and turned to winter,
to some grey monochrome, much like this metre,
with no gold in it. So, I saw my toil
as a seedy little yard of scrub and root
that gripped for good, and what took in that soil,
was the cheap flower that you see at my foot,
the coarsest, commonest, toughest, nondescript,
resilient violet with its white spot centre.

Parades, Parades

There's the wide desert, but no one marches
except in the pads of old caravans,
there is the ocean, but the keels incise
the precise, old parallels,
there's the blue sea above the mountains
but they scratch the same lines
in the jet trails,
so the politicians plod
without imagination, circling
the same sombre gardens
with its fountain dry in the forecourt,
the gri-gri palms desicating
dung pods like goats,
the same lines rule the White Papers,
the same steps ascend Whitehall,
and only the name of the fool changes
under the plumed white cork-hat
for the Independence Parades
revolving around, in calypso,
to the brazen joy of the tubas.

Why are the eyes of the beautiful
and unmarked children
in the uniforms of the country
bewildered and shy,
why do they widen in terror
of the pride drummed into their minds?
Were they truer, the old songs,
when the law lived far away,
when the veiled queen, her girth
as comfortable as cushions,

upheld the orb with its stern admonitions?
We wait for the changing of statues,
for the change of parades.

Here he comes now, here he comes!
Papa! Papa! With his crowd,
the sleek, waddling seals of his Cabinet,
trundling up to the dais,
as the wind puts its tail between
the cleft of the mountain, and a wave
coughs once, abruptly.
Who will name this silence
respect? Those forced, hoarse hosannas
awe? That tin-ringing tune
from the pumping, circling horns
the New World? Find a name
for that look on the faces
of the electorate. Tell me
how it all happened, and why
I said nothing.

Midsummer, Tobago

Broad sun-stoned beaches.

White heat.
A green river.

A bridge,
scorched yellow palms

from the summer-sleeping house
drowsing through August.

Days I have held,
days I have lost,

days that outgrow, like daughters,
my harbouring arms.

Egypt, Tobago

for N. M.

There is a shattered palm
on this fierce shore,
its plumes the rusting helm-
et of a dead warrior.

Numb Antony, in the torpor
stretching her inert
sex near him like a sleeping cat,
knows his heart is the real desert.

Over the dunes
of her heaving,
to his heart's drumming
fades the mirage of the legions,

across love-tousled sheets,
the triremes fading.
At the carved door of her temple
a fly wrings its message.

He brushes a damp hair
away from an ear
as perfect as a sleeping child's.
He stares, inert, the fallen column.

He lies like a copper palm
tree at three in the afternoon
by a hot sea
and a river, in Egypt, Tobago.

Her salt marsh dries in the heat
where he foundered
without armour.
He exchanged an empire for her beads of sweat,

the uproar of arenas,
the changing surf
of senators, for
this silent ceiling over silent sand –

this grizzled bear, whose fur,
moulting, is silvered –
for this quick fox with her
sweet stench. By sleep dismembered,

his head
is in Egypt, his feet
in Rome, his groin a desert
trench with its dead soldier.

He drifts a fringer
through her stiff hair
crisp as a mare's fountaining tail.
Shadows creep up the palace tile.

He is too tired to move;
a groan would waken
trumpets, one more gesture,
war. His glare,

a shield
reflecting fires,
a brass brow that cannot frown
at carnage, sweats the sun's force.

It is not the turmoil
of autumnal lust,
its treacheries, that drove
him, fired and grimed with dust,

this far, not even love,
but a great rage without
clamour, that grew great
because its depth is quiet;

it hears the river
of her young brown blood,
it feels the whole sky quiver
with her blue eyelid.

She sleeps with the soft engine of a child,

that sleep which scythes
the stalks of lances, fells the
harvest of legions
with nothing for its knives,
that makes Caesars,

sputtering at flies,
slapping their foreheads
with the laurel's imprint,
drunkards, comedians.

All-humbling sleep, whose peace
is sweet as death,
whose silence has
all the sea's weight and volubility,

who swings this globe by a hair's trembling breath.

Shattered and wild and
palm-crowned Antony,
rusting in Egypt,
ready to lose the world,
to Actium and sand,

everything else
is vanity, but this tenderness
for a woman not his mistress
but his sleeping child.

The sky is cloudless. The afternoon is mild.

Upstate

A knife blade of cold air keeps prying
the bus window open. The spring country
won't be shut out. The door to the john
keeps banging. There're a few of us:
a stale-drunk or stoned woman in torn jeans,
a Spanish-American salesman, and, ahead,
a black woman folded in an overcoat.
Emptiness makes a companionable aura
through the upstate villages – repetitive,
but crucial in their little differences
of fields, wide yards with washing, old machinery – where
    people live
with the highway's patience and flat certainty.

Sometimes I feel sometimes
the Muse is leaving, the Muse is leaving America.
Her tired face is tired of iron fields,
its hollows sing the mines of Appalachia,
she is a chalk-thin miner's wife with knobbled elbows,
her neck tendons taut as banjo strings,
she who was once a freckled palomino with a girl's mane
galloping blue pastures plinkety-plunkety,
staring down at a tree-stunned summer lake,
when all the corny calendars were true.
The departure comes over me in smoke
from the far factories.

But were the willows lyres, the fanned-out pollard willows
with clear translation of water into song,
were the starlings as heartbroken as nightingales,
whose sorrow piles the looming thunderhead

over the Catskills, what would be their theme?
The spring hills are sun-freckled, the chaste white barns
     flash
through screening trees the vigour of her dream,
like a white plank bridge over a quarrelling brook.
Clear images! Direct as your daughters
in the way their clear look returns your stare,
unarguable and fatal –
no, it is more sensual.
I am falling in love with America.

I must put the cold small pebbles from the spring
upon my tongue to learn her language,
to talk like birch or aspen confidently.
I will knock at the widowed door
of one of these villages
where she will admit me like a broad meadow,
like a blue space between mountains,
and holding her arms at the broken elbows
brush the dank hair from a forehead
as warm as bread or as a homecoming.

Midsummer

L

I once gave my daughters, separately, two conch shells
that were dived from the reef, or sold on the beach, I
    forget.
They use them as doorstops or bookends, but their wet
pink palates are the soundless singing of angels.
I once wrote a poem called 'The Yellow Cemetery',
when I was nineteen. Lizzie's age. I'm fifty-three.
These poems I heaved aren't linked to any tradition
like a mossed cairn; each goes down like a stone
to the seabed, settling, but let them, with luck, lie
where stones are deep, in the sea's memory.
Let them be, in water, as my father, who did watercolours,
entered his work. He became one of his shadows,
wavering and faint in the midsummer sunlight.
His name was Warwick Walcott. I sometimes believe
that his father, in love or bitter benediction,
named him for Warwickshire. Ironies
are moving. Now, when I rewrite a line,
or sketch on the fast-drying paper the coconut fronds
that he did so faintly, my daughters' hands move in mine.
Conches move over the sea floor. I used to move
my father's grave from the blackened Anglican headstones
in Castries to where I could love both at once –
the sea and his absence. Youth is stronger than fiction.

Cul de Sac Valley

I

A panel of sunrise
on a hillside shop
gave these stanzas
their stilted shape.

If my craft is blest;
if this hand is as
accurate, as honest
as their carpenter's,

every frame, intent
on its angles, would
echo this settlement
of unpainted wood

as consonants scroll
off my shaving plane
in the fragrant Creole
of their native grain;

from a trestle bench
they'd curl at my foot,
C's, R's, with a French
or West African root

from a dialect throng-
ing, its leaves unread
yet light on the tongue
of their native road;

but drawing towards
my pegged-out twine
with bevelled boards
of unpainted pine,

like muttering shale,
exhaling trees refresh
memory with their smell:
bois canot, bois campêche,

hissing: *What you wish
from us will never be,
your words is English,
is a different tree.*

Gros-Ilet

From this village, soaked like a grey rag in salt water,
a language came, garnished with conch shells,
with a suspicion of berries in its armpits
and elbows like flexible oars. Every ceremony commenced
in the troughs, in the middens, at the daybreak and the
    daydark funerals
attended by crabs. The odours were fortified
by the sea. The anchor of the islands went deep
but was always clear in the sand. Many a shark,
and often the ray, whose wings are as wide as sails,
rose with insomniac stare from the wavering corals,
and a fisherman held up a catfish like a tendrilled head.
And the night with its certain, inextinguishable candles
was like All Souls' Night upside down, the way a bat keeps
its own view of the world. So their eyes looked down,
    amused,
on us, and found we were walking strangely,
and wondered about our sense of balance, how we slept
as if we were dead, how we confused
dreams with ordinary things like nails, or roses,
how rocks aged quickly with moss,
the sea made furrows that had nothing to do with time,
and the sand started whirlwinds with nothing to do at all,
and the shadows answered to the sun alone.
And sometimes, like the top of an old tyre,
the black rim of a porpoise. Elpenor, you
who broke your arse, drunk, tumbling down the bulkhead,
and the steersman who sails, like the ray under the
    breathing waves,
keep moving, there is nothing here for you.

There are different candles and customs here, the dead
are different. Different shells guard their graves.
There are distinctions beyond the paradise
of our horizon. This is not the grape-purple Aegean.
There is no wine here, no cheese, the almonds are green,
the sea grapes bitter, the language is that of slaves.

To Norline

This beach will remain empty
for more slate-coloured dawns
of lines the surf continually
erases with its sponge,

and someone else will come
from the still-sleeping house,
a coffee mug warming his palm
as my body once cupped yours,

to memorise this passage
of a salt-sipping tern,
like when some line on a page
is loved, and it's hard to turn.

Salsa

The Morro has one eye, a slit.
It is hard grey stone, it is visored
like a scraped conquistador's helmet.
These days not much happens around it.
The palm frond rusts like a Castilian sword.

But there, the women have pomegranate skins
and eyes like black olives, and hair that shines
blue as a crow's wing, if they are Indians.
And the Indians there were Toltec and I forget
what else. But at the Ramada and Holiday Inns,
in water-plumed lounges with wet
plants, a salsa combo sings:

> '*Ay, caramba, gringo!*
> *Is getting like New York!*
> *or Miami, mi amigo, the lingo*
> *the hustling palm trees talk.*'

By the rusty and white walls of Cartagena,
a tree reads the palm of the sand,
but the lines fade quickly; 'Malagueña'
grates from a sun-straw-hatted band,
and a cockerel comes striding with its Quetzalcoatl
plumes, and the blackened palm fronds are cattle
barbecued by brigands, just like the Hilton's.
Every dusk there is the death rattle
of the shoal like maracas,
and a wind like a bamboo whistle,
xylophones of bones in the grass.

Saint Lucia's First Communion

At dusk, on the edge of the asphalt's worn-out ribbon,
in white cotton frock, cotton stockings, a black child
   stands.
First her, then a small field of her. Ah, it's First
   Communion!
They hold pink ribboned missals in their hands,

the stiff plaits pinned with their white satin moths.
The caterpillar's accordion, still pumping out the myth
along twigs of cotton from whose parted mouths
the wafer pods in belief without an 'if'!

So, all across Saint Lucia thousands of innocents
were arranged on church steps, facing the sun's lens,
erect as candles between squinting parents,
before darkness came on like their blinded saint's.

But if it were possible to pull up on the verge
of the dimming asphalt, before its headlights lance
their eyes, to house each child in my hands,
to lower the window a crack, and delicately urge

the last moth delicately in, I'd let the dark car
enclose their blizzard, and on some black hill,
their pulsing wings undusted, loose them in thousands to
   stagger
heavenward before it came on: the prejudice, the evil!

Omeros

Chapter XXVIII

III

Not where russet lions snarl on leaf-blown terraces,
or where ocelots carry their freckled shadows, or wind erases
Assyria, or where drizzling arrows hit the unflinching faces

of some Thracian phalanx winding down mountain passes,
but on a palm shore, with its vines and river grasses,
and stone barracoons, on brown earth, bare as their asses.

Yet they felt the sea-wind tying them into one nation
of eyes and shadows and groans, in the one pain
that is inconsolable, the loss of one's shore

with its crooked footpath. They had wept, not for
their wives only, their fading children, but for strange,
ordinary things. This one, who was a hunter,

wept for a sapling lance whose absent heft sang
in his palm's hollow. One, a fisherman, for an ochre
river encircling his calves; one a weaver, for the straw

fishpot he had meant to repair, wilting in water.
They cried for the little thing after the big thing.
They cried for a broken gourd. It was only later

that they talked to the gods who had not been there
when they needed them. Their whole world was moving,
or a large part of the world, and what began dissolving

was the fading sound of their tribal name for the rain,
the bright sound for the sun, a hissing noun for the river,
and always the word 'never', and never the word 'again'.

Glossary: reading the poems

These notes provide brief explanations of cultural, historical or literary references in the poems. In some cases you may want to do further research, particularly where a poem or sequence of poems hinges on knowledge of a particular myth or historical event. There are no notes on 'interpretation' or 'difficult words'. No notes appear on words which can be found in a dictionary. If you are to learn to be an experienced reader of poetry you need to develop a range of reading skills for yourself, rather than relying on the falsely 'authoritative' voice of an editor, giving interpretations of words and phrases. Look at the advice on page xv, designed to help you research references for yourself.

Parting is Such Sweet Sorrow

3 *Belshazzar's fiery script*   Belshazzar was a figure from the Old Testament. He was feasting when a mysterious human hand appeared and wrote a message on the wall. Daniel interpreted the message as meaning: 'You have been weighed in the balance and found wanting.' This seems to have been a sign from God, for that night Belshazzar was slain. In a famous painting, Rembrandt shows Belshazzar's feast, with the fiery writing glowing on the wall.

Bogyman

5 *Ambit*   a literary magazine.

Creosote

24 *outside dunny*   New Zealand term for an outside lavatory.

Stanton Drew

27 *Stanton Drew*   the Stanton Drew Stone Circles is a Bronze Age
site in Avon consisting of three circles. A local legend suggests
that the stones were guests at a wedding, who danced all night to
the tune of a strange fiddler, the devil in disguise, who turned
them to stone at dawn.

Mendip rim   the Mendips are a range of hills in Somerset, just south
of Bristol.

Casehistory: Alison (head injury)

28 *Like a Degas dancer's*   Degas was a French Impressionist painter.
He is particularly well known for his paintings of ballet dancers, on
stage and behind the scenes.

Earthed

31 *Browning, Hughes*   Robert Browning was a nineteenth-century
British poet. Ted Hughes is a modern British poet. Both wrote
famous poems about thrushes.

Not My Best Side

33 *Uccello*   St George and the Dragon: a painting by Uccello in the
National Gallery, showing St George wounding the dragon and
the princess tying her girdle round his neck, so that he can be led
off, conquered, into the town (see page 32).

Horticultural Show

35 *Persephone*   in Greek legend Persephone was carried off by Hades
(Pluto in Roman mythology) and forced to spend half the year
underground. The story represents the natural cycle of the
germination of seeds in the ground in the winter months,
followed by their rebirth as new shoots in the spring.

Fanfare

39 *Delectable Mountains*   *The Pilgrim's Progress* by John Bunyan (1628–88) is an allegorical journey towards spiritual salvation. The Delectable Mountains are one goal to be reached. The shepherds on the Mountains provide refreshment and help before the travellers continue on their hazardous journey towards the Celestial City.

Four Dogs

40 *Cerberus*   in Greek legend Cerberus was a monstrous dog guarding the entrance to the Underworld. In most sources he is described as having three heads. In several legends Cerberus appears as one of the tests or trials that a hero has to endure. Heracles has to bring Cerberus up from Hell as one of his Twelve Labours, Orpheus has to charm him with music to slip past him into the Underworld and Aeneas has to drug him with a cake soaked in honey and drugs.

    Anubis   the Ancient Egyptian god of the dead, represented by the figure of a man with the head of a jackal.

41 *El Perro (Goya)*   a drawing by the Spanish painter Goya (1746–1828). 'El Perro' means 'The Dog'.

At the Ferry

42 *Charon*   in Greek mythology Charon was the ferryman who took the dead in his boat across the river Styx, if the funeral rites had been performed and the fare paid. The fare was a coin in the mouth of the corpse. Because of this role, he has come to be associated with death.

The Passing of Alfred

44 *Alfred, Lord Tennyson*   a nineteenth-century poet, who was Poet Laureate to Queen Victoria. He is buried in Westminster Abbey.

Dig

52 *Troy*   the site of Troy was discovered in 1873 by a German archaeologist, Heinrich Schliemann. The great Greek poet Homer wrote an epic poem, the *Iliad*, about a city called Troy, ruled by King Priam, and about the wars between the Greeks and the Trojans. Schliemann identified the site of Troy as Hissarlik in north-west Turkey from Homer's descriptions in the *Iliad*. Troy was re-built by the Greeks and became the town of Ilium. Scamander was a river near Troy.

Mendere   Maeander was a large river flowing into the Aegean sea. It followed a tortuous course and hence the Greeks used its name to describe a winding pattern.

The Person's Tale

53 *S.T.C.*   Samuel Taylor Coleridge (1772–1834), an English Romantic poet. He is well known for 'The Rime of the Ancient Mariner', referred to in 'The Person's Tale'. The epigraph to 'The Person's Tale' is a note he wrote prefacing his famous poem 'Kubla Khan'. The epigraph tells us that Coleridge was disturbed by a visit from a 'person' and, his inspired mood interrupted, he never finished the poem. Amongst Coleridge's many personal problems was an addiction to opium, which began when he was prescribed narcotics during an illness.

Durham

56 *Quasimodo*   in *The Hunchback of Notre Dame*, a novel by Victor Hugo (1802–85), Quasimodo was a hunchback who lived in the cathedral and rang the bells.

Them & [uz]

60 *Demosthenes*   a Greek politician, who was said to have conquered a speech impediment by practising speeches against the noise of the sea, with a mouth full of pebbles. He went on to be acclaimed as the greatest of Greek orators.

mi 'art aches   John Keats' poem 'Ode to a Nightingale' begins 'My heart aches, and a drowsy numbness pains/My sense, as though of hemlock I had drunk'. Keats was born and lived in London and was, in this sense, a cockney. (See note on 'A Kumquat for John Keats'.)

61 *Wordsworth*   (1770–1850) a Romantic poet, who was born in Cockermouth in Cumbria and spent much of his life in the Lake District.

Long Distance

62 *JFK*   John F. Kennedy airport in New York.

Working

64 *getters, hurryer*   dialect words for jobs in the coal mines of the nineteenth century, when there was widespread use of child labour and women and no regulation of safety and working conditions. Getters cut the coal and hurryers pushed the coal corves, or baskets, along the colliery roads.

wordshift   arrangement of words.

inwit   old word for understanding, reason, inward sense.

gob   an old Northern coal-mining word for the space left after the coal has been extracted. Also, the mouth and speech.

Still

66 *Xenophon*   a Greek historian.

Brilliantine   hair oil.

Bringing Up

69 *Loiners*   a published collection of poetry by Harrison.

Remains

72 *Intimations of . . . immortality* William Wordsworth wrote a famous
poem 'Ode on Intimations of Immortality' (see note on 'Them &
[uz]' about Wordsworth).

A Kumquat for John Keats

73 *John Keats* John Keats was one of the great Romantic poets of the
late eighteenth and early nineteenth century. He was born in
1795 and died at a very young age, in 1821, of tuberculosis. He
was in love with Fanny Brawne and became engaged to her but
did not live to marry her. The Odes, for which he is most famous,
were written in 1819, two years before he died. There are
references in 'A Kumquat for John Keats' to the 'Ode on
Melancholy' and to 'Ode to a Nightingale'. It would be worth
reading these poems before studying 'A Kumquat for John Keats'.

75 *Lemprière* John Lemprière (1765–1824) was the writer of a
classical dictionary, which was widely used and ran to many
editions.

  a shirt of Nessus Nessus was a centaur who was killed by Heracles.
The blood on his shirt later killed Heracles. A fatal gift came to be
known as 'a shirt of Nessus'.

Cypress & Cedar

77 *'cracker' style* cracker is a term for poor whites in America.

78 *Phèdre* the chief character in the play by the French dramatist
Racine.

79 *Blue Guide, Fodor* tourist guides.

  Suwannee River and the Styx see biographical note on Tony
Harrison for Suwannee River. The Styx was the river in the
Underworld across which the souls of the dead were ferried by
Charon.

  Virgil in his Georgics III the **Georgics** were Virgil's pastoral poems,
about country life.

chelydrus   a Latin word, meaning a water serpent.

80 *Phlegethon's creek*   Phlegethon was one of the rivers of the Underworld. In Dante it is a river of boiling blood, into which sinners who have shed blood are thrown.

81 *Mimi's on cold stairs*   in the nineteenth-century opera by Puccini, 'La Bohème', Mimi's candle goes out on the stairs of the apartment in which she lives and she is assisted by the poet Rodolpho who falls in love with her. It is a moment of high romance.

82 *Tvashti*   Tvashtri or Twashtri is a figure from Hindu mythology, who was the most skilful of all workers and artisans. In the Rig Veda he carries an iron axe and forges the thunderbolts of the storm god Indra. He is invoked for blessings and prosperity.

Rig Veda   an ancient Vedic religious work, consisting of a collection of hymns addressed to various gods and divine powers. Hinduism had its roots in Vedic religions.

The Other House

99 *'Ignis fatuus'*   in Latin it literally means 'foolish fire'. Its modern meaning is false hope or plan. Stevenson may have been thinking of a seventeenth-century writer, John Wilmot, Earl of Rochester, who commented on Reason being an 'ignis fatuus of the mind'.

Elegy

101 *'Trout'*   Franz Peter Schubert's Trout piano quintet is particularly well known. Schubert was born near Vienna in 1797, the son of a schoolteacher. He started composing as a young boy and became one of the earliest and greatest of the Romantic composers.

lachrimae rerum   in the **Aeneid**, the Roman poet Virgil wrote 'Sunt lacrimae rerum et mentem mortalia tangunt' meaning 'Human deeds have their tears, and mortality touches the heart.'

movable doh   doh is a keynote of the musical scale. Fixed doh is C but movable doh can be any note.

Steinways   a Steinway is an expensive and beautiful piano made by the Steinway firm of piano makers.

Schirmer's Editions, Peters Editions   editions of sheet music.

in excrucio   in extreme pain.

Stone Fig

103 *Platonic Idea of Fig*   beyond the existence of real figs that one can eat, there is the essence of fig, the idea of fig.

Journal Entry: Impromptu in C Minor

109 *Schubert*   see note on 'Elegy'.

Eros

112 *Eros*   the Greek god of Love, who was known as Cupid in Roman mythology. Eros is presented in some sources as powerful and cruel whilst in others his playfulness, youth and beauty are given more emphasis.

Ruins of a Great House

114 *Browne: Urn Burial*   Sir Thomas Browne was a seventeenth-century religious and philosophical writer. His **Hydriotaphia**, or **Urn Burial**, was a discussion of burial customs in different ages and countries and contained reflections on death and immortality which were solemn and eloquent.

disjecta membra   in his Satires, the Roman poet Horace wrote: 'Tempora certa modosque, et quod prius ordine verbum est/ Posterius facia, praeponens ultima primis . . . / Invenias etiam disiecti membra poetae.' This means: 'Take away the rhythm and the metre, and put the first word last and the last first; still the dispersed limbs are those of a poet.'

155

Great House   when European colonisers came to the West Indies they made their wealth out of large plantations, worked by black slaves. After emancipation the owners remained and still employed black servants to work on the estates. The owners lived in large houses on the estates, which came to be known as 'the Great Houses' and this name became symbolic of the whole colonial power of the white owners.

Faulkner's south   William Faulkner (1897–1962) was an American novelist who wrote about the Deep South, examining the society and the reasons for its decay. He explored the history of slavery and the Civil War and their influences on the modern Southern experience. His vision was one of greed and guilt putting a curse on the land.

115 *Kipling*   Rudyard Kipling (1865–1936) was an English writer, who is most famous for his stories and poems about India. He was intensely patriotic and was a strong believer in the British Empire.

Hawkins, Walter Raleigh, Drake   were all seafaring men living in the reign of Queen Elizabeth I. They all undertook voyages to the West Indies or the Spanish Main, to exploit the riches of the New World, and were therefore part of the history of England becoming a colonial power in the West Indies.

Donne   John Donne was a seventeenth-century clergyman, poet and thinker. In his ***Devotions*** he wrote: 'No man is an island, entire of itself; every man is a piece of the continent, a part of the main. If a clod be washed away, Europe is the less, as well as if a manor of thy friend's or thine own were. . .'

Albion   the Greek and Roman name for Britain, now used as a poetic term for it.

Laventille

118 *the middle passage*   during the African slave trade, slaves were transported by ship across the Atlantic, in appalling, inhumane conditions. This part of their journey has been termed 'the middle passage'.

Mass Man

121 *mass man*   Carnival is an important event in Trinidadian life and
people spend months preparing their costumes for the
masquerade. Masqueraders are sometimes called 'mas men'.
However mass has other meanings, which the poet plays on.

your penitential morning   the two days of Carnival are immediately
followed by Ash Wednesday, the beginning of the Catholic
season of Lent, when there is fasting and prayer as penance for
sins.

Homecoming: Anse La Raye

122 *Helen*   in Homer's *Iliad*, Helen was the beautiful wife of Menelaus
of Sparta, who was seduced by Paris and carried off to Troy, thus
starting the Trojan war. In the *Odyssey* Homer shows her
reconciled with Menelaus.

when her looms fade   a possible reference to Penelope, waiting for
the return of her husband Odysseus and weaving and unravelling
her weaving whilst she waits.

entering your needle's eye   in the New Testament, Matthew 19:24,
Jesus says: 'It is easier for a camel to go through the eye of a
needle, than for a rich man to enter into the kingdom of God.'

Another Life: Chapter 2 (II)

125 *the Singer*   a make of sewing machine.

jour marron   a type of bus.

Victrola cabinet   a wind-up gramophone in a wooden cabinet.

126 *Warwick and Alix*   the names of Walcott's father and mother.

Pears Cyclopedia   Walcott is remembering the illustration of a
beautiful white child that appeared in the encyclopaedia and
became a very familiar image for several generations.

Another Life: Chapter 15 (I)

128 *Christie, Karenina* women of film and fiction, who had to endure tragic partings with their lovers on station platforms. Julie Christie played the female lead in *Doctor Zhivago* and Anna Karenina was the heroine of Tolstoy's novel of the same name.

The Harvest

129 *pouis* trees with a golden blossom.

Parades, Parades

130 *the veiled queen* Queen Victoria, the ruler of the British Empire.

131 *Papa! Papa!* Papa Doc was the name given to the tyrannical ruler of Haiti, an island in the Caribbean.

Midsummer, Tobago

132 *Tobago* Walcott lived in Trinidad and Tobago while working on the *Trinidad Guardian.*

Egypt, Tobago

133 *Antony* his full name was Mark Antony. He was a Roman politician and soldier, who supported Julius Caesar. After Caesar's death he formed a ruling triumvirate with Lepidus and Octavian. He later commanded the forces of the Eastern Empire, during which time he had a liaison with Cleopatra, Queen of Egypt, who had previously been Julius Caesar's mistress. He then married Octavian's sister but later returned to Cleopatra and was suspected of disloyalty by Octavian. Octavian went to war with him and defeated him at sea, at the battle of Actium. Antony returned to Egypt and committed suicide.

Cul de Sac Valley (I)

141 *bois canot, bois campêche*   French Creole words for two types of wood.

Gros-Ilet

142 *All Souls' Night*   a date in the Christian calendar, 2 November.

Elpenor   in Homer's *Odyssey*, Elpenor was one of Odysseus' crew members, who was young and foolish. He broke his neck falling off the roof of Circe's palace in his sleep. His ghost met Odysseus in the underworld and begged for cremation and a barrow with his oar on top.

143 *Aegean*   one of the seas surrounding Greece.

Salsa

144 *the Morro*   Morro castle is a fort at the entrance to the harbour of Havana, Cuba. It was erected by the Spanish in 1589 to protect the city from buccaneers and was captured by the British in 1762.

Cartagena   Cartagena is a port in Colombia, on the Caribbean sea. It was founded in 1533 and became the treasure city of the Spanish Main, where precious stones and minerals from the New World awaited shipment to Spain. It was guarded by twenty-nine stone forts but suffered many invasions, including one by Sir Francis Drake. It was one of the first towns to declare absolute independence from Spain in 1811.

Omeros Chapter XXVIII (III)

146 *Assyria*   the ancient empire of Mesopotamia.

Thracian phalanx   Thrace was an ancient kingdom on the Greek mainland. A phalanx was a line of soldiers, in close formation, preparing for battle.

Working on the anthology

☐ Make a chart of themes dealt with by more than one poet in the anthology. List the poems under the heading of each theme. Read all of the poems dealing with a particular theme and explore the poets' treatment of that theme, by comparing the ideas and the style in which they are presented. (Use the theme list on page xiii to help you.)

② Make a selection of the poems you have read and liked, for different purposes, e.g.

- a selection to introduce a lower sixth student to the anthology;
- a selection to be read at a poetry reading for other A Level students/parents;
- a selection of your favourite poems.

Write a justification for your selection, relating it to the particular audience you have chosen. Present your selection to other students in the group.

③ Work as a seminar group.

Decide on some key questions or issues about a poet, or the anthology as a whole. Give a task to small groups or individuals to prepare for the following lesson, so that there are a number of presentations to the rest of the group. Presentations can be aided by handouts, use of overhead projectors or other visual aids.

④ Look at these extracts from reviews of collections of poems by the poets in this anthology. For each poet, make a list of statements from the reviews that you agree or disagree with. Find evidence from the poems to justify your view on each statement. Discuss the statements in a group, arguing your case and drawing on your evidence.

Fleur Adcock

Reviews of *Selected Poems:*

'This is my laconic style,' Fleur Adcock says to a dead lover in the less-than-laconic 'Poem Ended by Death'. Most of her best poems preserve a decorum in the face of death, disease, pain. So do most of her worst. Reading through her **Selected Poems** you realise that the dividing line between containment and contentment is narrower than at first seems possible. She is a shapely poet, but the shapes often seem pre-determined; it is as though the experiences she sets out to record come pre-packed, neatly ordered, consigned to the reader in exact measure. . .

. . . But running through her work is a wit that hones itself, coolly and deliberately, on rebarbative material. When this is successful, the result is a poem of unique value, and such poems occur with increased frequency as the volume goes on.

John Lucas, **New Statesman,** 13 January 1984

Fleur Adcock, born in New Zealand, has lived and worked in England for the last twenty years. Her verse is quiet, crisp, reasonable, and compact. If it lacks excitement – and it does – then I can readily imagine her claiming that as a virtue. It does not lack feeling and intelligence. The work in her **Selected Poems** (£7.95, Oxford University Press) presents a record of solid achievement, and it is good to note a certain progress underlying it. On the technical level this could be described as a movement away from strict classical forms in search of something that will approximate to the twists and turns of common speech. This development seems mostly inspired by the poet's awareness that she now has, quite simply, more to say than when she began, so that it is no accident that the newer work admits a greater complexity both of thought and feeling. The overriding tone is thoroughly anti-romantic.

Robert Nye, **The Times,** 27 October 1983

Her imagination thrives on what threatens her peace of mind, and only when she is unguarded can these threats have their full creative effect. Hence the importance of bed: it is the place where the elegant, artful barriers that she builds from day to day are most easily overthrown. Passion and sickness are voluntary and involuntary ways of lessening – if not actually losing – self-control, and dreams themselves are direct dispatches from a side of the mind that cannot be manipulated or tidied up. . .

Poem after poem in the book rehearses similar or parallel dichotomies: between high hopes and bad dreams, between fact and fantasy, between innocence and disillusionment, and between what can be observed and what can be imagined. Not surprisingly, these tensions are reflected in the tone as well as the themes of her work.

Andrew Motion, **Times Literary Supplement,** 2 September 1983

There are plenty of 'I am's' and 'I was': the persona (because the 'I' is as much a persona as any other literary invention) is that of a self-observing, feminine loner, talking quietly and intelligently about her place in the world (or her lack of a place) and addressing many of her poems to friends, relations, lovers, sons, etc. It's like reading someone's private letters. Sometimes the shared intimacy is fascinating (when interestingly 'intimate' things are happening), sometimes it's less so (because the reader can't always know the Alistairs, Marilyns, Jims, Megs, Andrews, Gregorys etc, that are part of her circle).

Peter Bland, **London Magazine,** October 1985

Review of **High Tide in the Garden**

Fleur Adcock's poems suggest not only a woman's sensibility and preoccupations but a woman's voice – as distinctly as handwriting can suggest a female hand. She is (if I can speak loosely for the fraternity) better than most of us. She always writes well. She seems gifted with that slightly detached female intelligence that can martial even the most wayward feelings and make verbal sense and shape of them. But her poetic virtues are also her poetic limitations. She lacks the will, the passion, the ebullience, buoyancy, egotism on which great or strongly original structures are flung up.

She is least engaging when she is merely accomplished, when she seems to write out of an idea rather than out of the conjugations of actual pain and pleasure.

C. K. Stead

U. A. Fanthorpe

Reviews of *Standing To*

She is an erudite poet, rich in experience and haunted by the classical past. Though Charon and Sisyphus and Alfred have walk-on parts in her poetry, she is fully at home in the world of the turbulent NHS, the decayed academies, and all the draughty corners of the abandoned Welfare State. Reading her well-stocked book is rather like settling down with a good novel: there are so many reminders of the way we live now.

But she offers more than this: she is a good phrase-maker, and a humane commentator. Her instances are seldom outré, but the yokings she suggests are full of surprises.

Peter Porter, *Observer,* 7 November 1982

Who, though, will move you, going straight for the emotions? Unhesitatingly, I name U. A. Fanthorpe as the poet who can suddenly hit you below the heart. Her **Side Effects** *(1978, Harry Chambers/Peterloo) struck an assured, new note which* **Standing To** *(Chambers/Peterloo £3.00) continues without a tremor. A former schoolmistress, she now works full-time in a Bristol hospital and began publishing poems at the age of fifty.*

I read her with trepidation, fearing from the poems' homely titles that it would all end with a dreadful bump. But it never did, and the human observation, pathos, and imagination of her work are open gifts to anyone. Hospital life gives her some cues, but her range goes far wider, from fancies on London's lost rivers and Uccello's paintings to her tribute, which moved me quite deeply, to Virgil. 'Are there others like me?' she asks in **Standing To**'s *title poem. 'Encoding what they see, Abandoned by Higher Command?' Indeed there are, but none quite like this poetic sentry on watch.*

Robert Lane Fox, *Financial Times,* 8 January 1983

Reviews of **Selected Poems**

Ms. Fanthorpe is as English as the garden fete and cucumber sandwiches, the Beeb and John Betjeman (one would expect to see her on Greenham Common or collecting fossils in the Burren) and her inspired sorties on the layers of untruths that mask the human face makes a reading and re-reading of her poetry a voyage of discovery and identification. Ms. Fanthorpe gets to the intuitive core of things, making us see the poetry in the everyday.

Michael Dromey, **Cork Examiner,** 26 June 1986

Above all, she is interested in people and this results in her frequent use of the dramatic monologue. Capturing another person's voice convincingly is not easy, and Fanthorpe gets mixed results from the form.

. . . U. A. Fanthorpe's failures testify to one of her great strengths – the courage to take risks. Her poems display a wide sympathy, a sharp eye, and an informed, critical intelligence.

Simon Rae, **Times Literary Supplement,** 7 November 1986

This juxtaposition of order and experience . . . is central. It involves the modesty of real attentiveness and results in poems which are not only accessible and clear-sighted, but also combine distance and compassion, coolness and warmth, head and heart. Poise does not, however, mean bloodlessness: U. A. Fanthorpe is clear about her allegiances and dislikes and condemns with a fine asperity the kind of bogus authority which relies on mystique, whether medical, academic or linguistic. She is equally good at confounding other received truths and, along with them, our expectations.

Arts South West, No. 38, July/August 1986

Reviews of **A Watching Brief**

This is a poetry that aims to sit on the page as naturally as prose, and to be as inclusive as prose. It is a deliberately democratic art, and has a feminist impulse behind it too.

Roger Garfitt, **London Magazine,** August/September 1988

*It is understanding, undemanding, truthful and trite. When she tries to be instructive, Fanthorpe can be ghastly. . . But there are poems in **A Watching Brief** that show the light-hearted, light-metred Fanthorpe still well ahead. . .*

Michael Hulse, *Observer*

Tony Harrison

Reviews of *Selected Poems*

There is in these poems a striking mixture of emotional vigour and patness. . . Some of the attempts in these poems to blend the parents' Yorkshire speech with the stylish sweep of Harrison's own metrical fluencies seem affected or patronising, or else over-strenuously willed or wilful. But at their best the poems in this idiom have a tender truthfulness; and Leeds, the place where he grew up, is a vividly evoked presence throughout the volume.

Claude Rawson

*Tony Harrison's **Selected Poems** (Viking, 204pp, £9.95; paperback, £3.50) is to be welcomed. There is no question but that he is 'one of the few modern poets who actually has the gift of composing poetry', as James Fenton somewhat confusedly puts it on the dustcover – but one sees what is meant. Here is to be found the complete text of Mr Harrison's grittily lapidary versions of the poems of Palladas, besides previously uncollected pieces like the splendid 'A Kumquat for John Keats'.*

The heart of the book is, of course, the magnificent autobiographic Meredithian sonnets of his work in progress, 'A School of Eloquence' – though for all their power one gets a bit bored with the aggressive working-class stance that seems superimposed upon, rather than integral to, many of them.

What is remarkable is Mr Harrison's amazing ability to transmute common speech – as when he uses a recently-discovered pencilled inscription, left by Victorian workmen behind wallpaper in Dove Cottage, for the final line of a sonnet, thus demonstrating its poetry: 'Our heads will be happen cold when this is found.'

David Wright, *Sunday Telegraph*

*Tony Harrison has been hailed by a specimen-hunter as 'the first genuine working-class poet England has produced this century'. His **Selected Poems** establishes that the important thing is simply that he is a genuinely talented poet – an original. His voice throughout this collection is quite distinctive – a heavily stressed iambic metre, with emphatic monosyllables and rhymes, varied by bursts of colloquial or unexpectedly recondite vocabulary. He also stands out by virtue of working in regular forms – such as a 16-line sonnet. His subjects are predominantly his own North Country family background, and his subsequent travels away from it, both geographically (poems here on Beverly Hills and Prague, as well as Durham and Newcastle), and linguistically, in an estranged speech.*

His puns and rhymes lapse sometimes into whimsy and doggerel, but his rumbustious energy makes this book very winning (and in paperback, a bargain).

David Sexton, *Financial Times*

*Milton and Keats are among the stars that Tony Harrison steers by. Why then does his **Selected Poems** (Viking £9.95. Penguin £3.50 pp208) put me in mind of Kipling? It has to do with the pace of his poems, their lack of repose, the sudden clarification in images brilliantly rendered. It has to do with the emphatic rhyming, the bold awkwardness of technique, the use of dialects, the rich excess. Then there's the geographical and thematic range – evident not only in the exotica of working-class Leeds but in dedications such as 'for Miroslav Holub, Havana, 1969' and 'for Jane Fonda, Leningrad, 1978' (a sonnet about clitoridectomy). He's been around; that's part of what the poems are about. Then there's the button-holing manner, the narrative content, the insistent maleness of voice.*

And the poems are steeped in politics. Harrison addresses not his political friends but agnostics and foes. He preaches to convert. He's praised for exploiting elements which 'genteel practitioners' are shy of – bold statement, explicit sexual content, a native dialect at once expressive and crude. When his work was not properly heeded, he had the excuse that no one seemed to be listening. When people started liking what they heard, he tended to play it again in different keys. . .

Harrison sets out to speak for those who haven't had 'a voice' in the world of power and whose silence has meant repression. He speaks for them, not to them. Some critics claim he is easily 'accessible'. It's not a claim he would make.

Michael Schmidt, **The Sunday Times,** 11 November 1984

Anne Stevenson

Reviews of **Selected Poems**

*When one glances rapidly through Anne Stevenson's **Selected Poems 1956– 1986** virtuosity and sophistication are the qualities which first spring to mind. These are deceptive and rather like the sparkle the sun sends down on the sea; the depths are concealed. Anne Stevenson is at times a virtuoso writer but this is largely because she can command a quite remarkably wide range of cadences and verse-forms. . . . These poems are lyrical, wise, but, above all, passionate.*

Anne Stevenson's range of subject-matter is wide and she can write with mastery about love, being a parent and other human relationships. She is an almost raptly attentive observer of Nature; she is alert to every change of season. . . . Her writing is spare yet sensuous, tangible but also thoughtful.

Elizabeth Jennings, **The Independent,** 14 May 1987

Work from the past decade reinforces a sense of Anne Stevenson as a writer of refined perception with philosophical or meditative leanings. Not really an urban poet, nor a pastoral one, she is most at home in the country, outdoors, but with a cottage nearby to return to.

Alfred Corn, **New York Times Book Review,** Sunday, 15 November 1987

*To read Anne Stevenson's **Selected Poems** (1987) chronologically is to realise an emergent pattern in her work. Hers is a spiritual search undertaken, frustrated, buried, resurrected and tried again, every time in a different key.*

Dewi Stephen Jones, **New Welsh Review,** Autumn 1989, No. 6

She has weight. She manages to be conversational, accessible, easy to read aloud, while remaining capable of taking language to a purpose beyond the merely conversational. She doesn't 'poeticize', doesn't deliberately attempt to dazzle, but is always exact, precise, using her toolbox to dissect the meaning of her subjects. Her concerns are often domestic: house and garden, flowers and birds, the changing seasons. She is profoundly concerned with the natural world, but somehow she is not a nature poet, never surrendering her discrete control in the face of that beauty, but sitting, elegantly poised within her perception, intelligently noting the movement of growth and life.

What is more likely to disturb her detachment and unsettle her emotions comes from inside: from language and imagination and from the turbulence of involvement in relationships infused with love. As she grows older her engagement with these things remains as vivid, her concern as convincing, her technique as secure. She has produced an imposing body of work, and promises to deliver more in the future.

Martin Haslehurst, **The Anglo-Welsh Review**

Every poem has been wrought and thought through. None rely on the subject matter's intrinsic interest to carry them along. None rely on explanations, circumstances or footnotes. None rely on the reader's erudition or initiation. None rely on being of topical concern politically or socially. None rely on being shocking or sensational. None rely on conformity to any fashionable school of style or lifestyle, theory or anti-theory, structure or de-structure or re-structure. None rely on any ism of politics, literature or religion. None even rely on Anne's own personal story or achievement, background or character. The poem is the thing.

Of course this does not imply that the poems are detached from human life in the real world. That they do not rely on extraneous contingencies for their merit or appeal, does not mean they they are not riddled through and through with the essential marks of life, whether physical or metaphysical, emotional or intellectual, geographical or socio-psychological.

Tessa Ransford, **Lines Review,** December 1987

Derek Walcott

Walcott is essentially a poet of grace, not so much a carpenter as a sculptor of light . . . Walcott is a magnificent descriptive poet: the surveyor and unacknowledged legislator of the West Indies. But this power extends far beyond the islands. If you read no other poetry this year you should read him.

George Szirtes

Walcott is neither a traditionalist nor a modernist. He belongs to no school . . . He can be naturalistic, expressionistic, surrealistic, imagistic, hermetic, confessional – you name it. He simply has absorbed, the way whales do the plankton or a paintbrush the palette, all the stylistic idioms the north could offer, now he is on his own, and in a big way . . . He is the man by whom the English Language lives.

Joseph Brodsky, **Less than One: Selected Essays**

Review of *Collected Poems*

Early in his Collected Poems (Faber, 516pp, £20) the Caribbean poet Derek Walcott asks himself 'how choose/Between this Africa and the English tongue I love?' and after 500 pages he is still seeing his personal and poetic dilemmas in the same terms: 'And I whose ancestors were slave and Roman/have seen both sides of the imperial foam. . . .'

Not that the reader feels any sense of satiety – the historical, racial and linguistic struggles within the poet make for compelling reading, nowhere more so than in the book-length autobiographical poem 'Another Life'. Mr Walcott is a master of the grand style – of the reverberative associations of history, empire, sea-faring conquistadores – and also of the wry patois that sees through and undercuts such grandiloquence:

Arnold's Phoenecian trader reach
*   this far*
selling you half-dead batteries for
*   your car.*

His great strength is his fidelity to the complexity of his culture. One of Mr Walcott's most persistent themes is homesickness, his constant need to revisit, if only in the mind, the particularities of the places that formed him.

Sunday Telegraph, 28 December 1986

Review of **The Arkansas Testament**

> . . . his work is permeated by – made great by – a huge tear-stained sadness.
> Poem after poem celebrates some odyssey or other: Sea-routes, bus-rides, beach
> walks, lecture-tours, flights, walks, ruminations, voyages, island-hops. This
> recurring longing for a centre is his greatest theme.
>
> Waldemar Januszczak, **Guardian**, 9 July 1988

Review of **The Gulf and Other Poems**

> Derek Walcott, a West Indian with an acutely sensitive feel for the moral
> significance of place and landscape, writes a packed, complex, profusely
> metaphorical verse, held back from the edge of lushness by a deft metrical
> control and a terse vein of intelligence. He is able, within the flow of a sensuously
> heightened, almost visionary poetry, to analyse and discriminate precisely,
> drawing thought, image and sensation into a remarkably confident
> integration . . .
>
> The taut compactness of Mr Walcott's poetry (he almost always uses a short
> flexible metre) achieves a dazzling blending of image into image, and a
> simultaneous firmness of control over tone and movement. His verbal range is
> as rich and resourceful as that of any poet writing in English; but its colourful
> elegance is prevented from cloying by a strictly directed evolution of thought.

What kinds of writing?

Writing on this text may be of different kinds:

- ▣ Interim work, written during your study of the text, to begin to sort
  out your ideas. This kind of writing could be in the form of:
  - a reading log;
  - notes for a seminar;
  - preparation for class discussion;
  - exploratory essay-writing.

2   Creative writing of your own, to help you to become familiar with
    the choices available to the poet and the reasons behind them, e.g.

    - write a continuation of a poem in the same style;
    - write a parody of a poem, in which you exaggerate the typical
      features of the poem;
    - write your own poem on the same theme or your own poem
      in the same style as the poet.

3   Carefully planned writing at the end of studying a poet, or at the end
    of your study of the anthology, as a way of recording what you
    have learned and making considered judgements on the basis of
    detailed knowledge of the poems.

4   Timed essays, to prepare you for writing in an examination.

5   Many of the kinds of writing listed above may be used as coursework
    to be examined as part of a folder of work.

A few ideas for writing

1   Go back to your charts of themes or recurring patterns across the
    work of one or more poets. Use the charts to construct some
    possible titles for essays. Pool your titles with those of other
    students and discuss:

    - which titles you find most interesting;
    - whether each title is too narrow or too broad;
    - whether each title will allow scope for you to show your
      knowledge and the thinking that you have done about the text;
    - how individual titles could be adapted to make them more
      helpful and more likely to produce a good essay;
    - if you are studying this text as a set text, which titles would
      be likely to be the kinds of titles set by your exam board;

- if you are studying this text for coursework, which titles would make an interesting addition to your folder.

Select the best titles to share with the whole class.

Choose one of the titles and write the essay.

2 Turn some of the discussion ideas and work on individual poems on page 160 into writing, e.g.

- a selection of poems and introduction or rationale for the choice;

- an essay which takes as its title one of the statements by reviewers with which you strongly agree or disagree;

- a development of one of your seminar tasks into an essay;

- a piece of creative writing and a commentary explaining its relationship to the poem(s) upon which it was based, e.g. a continuation, a pastiche, a poem in the style of one of the poets.

3 Choose one or more poems that you think could lend themselves to being adapted to a different medium, e.g. a TV script, a play, a novel, a short story, a scene from a film. Try doing the adaptation and write a commentary explaining the decisions you took and what in the poem encouraged you to make those choices.

4 Choose three or four poems across the anthology that seem to you to have an interesting connection. The connection could be:

- thematic;

- stylistic;

- a similarity of voice;

- a similarity of mood;

e.g. the treatment of parenthood in 'With My Sons at Boarhills', 'Poem to My Daughter', 'For a Five Year Old' and 'Midsummer L'.

Write about the connections between the poems, exploring the differences as well as the similarities.

This educational edition first published 1993

Editorial material set in 10/12 point Gill Sans Light
Produced by Longman Singapore Publishers (Pte) Ltd
Printed in Singapore

ISBN 0 582 09713 4

Acknowledgements

We are grateful to the following for permission to reproduce
poems:

Jonathan Cape Ltd, a division of Random Century Group Ltd, for
'Missing the Sea' & 'Leventille' from The Castaway by Derek Walcott
(1969), 'Mass Man', 'Homecoming: Anse La Raye' & 'Guyana I' from
The Gulf by Derek Walcott (1975), 'Parades, Parades', 'The Harvest'
& 'Midsummer, Tobago' from Sea Grapes by Derek Walcott (1976);
Faber & Faber Ltd for 'Ruins of A Great House' from In A Green
Night by Derek Walcott (1962), 'Chapter 2 II' & 'Chapter 15 I' from
Another Life by Derek Walcott (1973), 'L' from Midsummer by

Derek Walcott (1984), 'Upstate' from *The Fortunate Traveller* by
Derek Walcott (1982), 'Cul de Sac Valley I', 'To Norline', 'Salsa',
'Gros-Ilet' & 'Saint Lucia's First Communion' from *The Arkansas
Testament* by Derek Walcott (1988), 'Chapter XXVII' & 'Chapter II
II' from *Omeros* by Derek Walcott (1990); the authors agent for
'Durham', 'National Trust', 'Them & (uz)', 'Working', 'Long Distance',
'Flood' 'Still', 'Background Material', 'Self Justification', 'Bringing Up',
'Lines to My Grandfathers', 'Remains', 'A Kumquat for John Keats' &
'Cyprus and Cedar' from *Selected Poems* by Tony Harrison
(Penquin, 1984), copyright Tony Harrison; Oxford University Press
for 'For a Five-Year-Old', 'Parting is Such Sweet Sorrow', 'Bogyman',
'A Surprise in the Peninsula', 'Happy Ending', 'Grandma', 'Stewart
Island', 'Please Identify Yourself', 'Script', 'Things', 'Prelude',
'Accidental', 'A Walk in the Snow', 'House-talk', 'Instead of an
Interview', 'Crab', 'Blue Grass' from *Selected Poems* by Fleur Adcock
(1983) & 'Creosote' & 'Toads' from *Time-Zones* by Fleur Adcock
(1991), 'The Marriage', 'With My Sons at Boarhills', 'If I could Paint
Essences', 'The Garden', 'Buzzard and Alder' from *Selected Poems
1956-1986* by Anne Stevenson (1987), 'Taking Down the
Christmas Tree', 'Making Poetry', 'In the Tunnel of Summers', 'Spring
Song of the Poet-Housewife', 'A Prayer to Live with Real People'
from *The Fiction-Makers* by Anne Stevenson (1985), 'The Other
House', 'Elegy', 'What I Miss', 'Welsh Pastoral', 'Stone Fig', 'From the
Motorway', 'Journal Entry: Impromptu in C Minor', 'Eros' from *The
Other House* by Anne Stevenson (1990), 'The Three' & 'Poem to My
Daughter' from *Minute by Glass Minute* by Anne Stevenson (1982);
Peterloo Poets Ltd for 'The List', 'Casehistory: Alison (head injury)',
'Stanton Drew', 'Earthed', 'Not My Best Side', 'Horticultural Show'
from *Side Effects* by U A Fanthorpe (1978), 'Stations Underground:
Fanfare, Four Dogs, At the Ferry, The Passing of Alfred', 'Half-term',
'The Contributors', 'Hang-gliders in January', 'Father in the Railway
Buffet' from *Standing To* by U A Fanthorpe (1982), 'Growing Up',
'Dig' & 'The Person's Tale' from *Voices Off* by U A Fanthorpe (1984).

We are grateful to the National Gallery for permission to reproduce
the photograph on page 32.